T0143009

Second in the Courtship of God Series

Betrothed
.TO THE
King *Relationships
that Succeed*

Jim and Shelvy Wyatt

WESTBOW
PRESS®
A DIVISION OF THOMAS NELSON
& ZONDERVAN

WestBow Press books may be ordered through booksellers or by contacting:

WestBow Press
A Division of Thomas Nelson & Zondervan
1663 Liberty Drive
Bloomington, IN 47403
www.westbowpress.com
1 (866) 928-1240

ISBN: 978-1-9736-0030-5 (sc)
ISBN: 978-1-9736-0031-2 (hc)
ISBN: 978-1-9736-0029-9 (e)

Library of Congress Control Number: 2017912525

Print information available on the last page.

WestBow Press rev. date: 9/11/2017

Dedication

To Paul and Gretel Haglin—
Role models of a successful marriage,
Ministers of the faith
…and friends.

Acknowledgements

We wish to thank Steve Beane for copy-editing this book. His suggestions helped to bring greater understanding and clarity. Thank you Steve, for taking so much time to help us bring this work to book form.

Thank you Lisa Leach, for your labor of love and professional assistance in the details. Couldn't have done it without you.

Thank you to our dear friends, Sharon and Bruce, who once again let us use their beach house for a quiet place to write.

Thank you and blessings to Leslie for her encouragement and support; the Lord told you exactly what we needed.

Thank you to Lindsay Blaze, our lady-in-waiting who graces our cover.

Thank you to the many that were touched by The Courtship Of God and encouraged us to write a second book.

Thank you to our Lord for the many who have come to us for prayer and counseling for over 30 years. What an encouragement to witness the Holy Spirit working as Spiritual Detective to help us discern root woundings. And the joy of watching the Wonderful Counselor healing and transforming lives!

Thank you to our teachers and mentors, John and Paula Sandford; also Fletch and Betty Fletcher. We love and appreciate your sacrifices as you've pioneered this ministry to the brokenhearted.

Contents

Foreword

In this second volume of *The Courtship of God* series, Shelvy and Jim Wyatt have written a magnificent book. It will exult your heart with wondrous revelations, and in the same moment flay you alive, as the Holy Spirit shows you how far you are from living the simple truths Jim and Shelvy live routinely, every day.

Jim and Shelvy write alternately, sharing fascinating stories from their counseling sessions and from their own lives (without breaking confidentiality). They open our eyes to see the ever-present grace and providence of God. He is always there to love us—even in the pits of life. Valuable lessons about inner healing are to be learned in the many testimonial stories of people healed by counsel and prayer.

They teach, by sharing from their own lives, how to ponder what God may be doing in each event in our lives. They reveal how to use journals prophetically and for intercession.

The Bible comes alive as they quote Scripture throughout the book. You will come away with regained hunger to continually delve into His Word.

Every opinion and statement in the book is documented scripturally, a valuable lesson in itself. Consequently, it would be difficult to find something to quarrel about theologically or biblically. The book is safe to read, but dangerous to complacency that often besets us all!

The Courtship of God series purposely does not tell a consecutive story. Shelvy and Jim jump from testimonies of healing, to stories of their own experiences, to chapters extolling the glory of God, to sermonettes exhorting us to rekindle our first love. This keeps us on our toes, not knowing what to expect next.

You will find yourself caught up in the process of having courtship with God, which is Jim and Shelvy's basic purpose in writing the series.

May that be your experience! May you become unwilling to let anything deter you from responding to God's ever-loving courtship. I recommend reading and keeping the book nearby as a handy reference in the days and years to come.

Enjoy the book—and Him.

John Loren Sandford

Introduction

The book you're holding is the second in The Courtship of God Series. In this volume we look at what it means to be betrothed to the King.

> *Can it be that when we are in a love relationship with the King of Kings, we can learn to have healthy relationships in other areas of our lives?*

We explore some of those other relationships. How do we know when we have met the love of our lives? How can a marriage relationship be restored after betrayal and affairs? What about cyber-net relationships? Can they work? How do you get free in an abusive relationship? Is there life after divorce? Are some people destined to be single?

It's all about relationships!

In the first book of the Bible (*Genesis 1:26*) God said, "*Let **Us** make man in **Our_**image, according to **Our** likeness.*" Is He speaking of the Trinity? In the last book of the Bible, (*Revelation 22:17*) we see the invitation to the wedding feast: "*And the Spirit and the bride say, 'Come!' and let him who hears say, 'Come!'*"

It's all about relationships!

In Hosea 2:19 & 20 God renews His covenant with Israel, His people, His bride, the Church (of which we are a part), in the form of betrothal. "*I will **betroth** you to Me forever; yes, I will **betroth** you to Me in righteousness and justice. In lovingkindness and mercy; I will **betroth** you to Me in faithfulness, and you shall know the Lord.*" God is making a pledge to us that is permanent. A pledge of right living according to the will of God. He is just in all His ways toward us. His acts of kindness are motivated by love. He shows us pity that is undeserved, for He is compassionate and is being true to who He is in relationship to the one He loves. He makes a promise to us that we shall know an intimate relationship with Him.

It's all about relationships!

In the other volumes in the Courtship of God series (look for future releases) you will find yet more stories of this marvelous courtship as it touches other stages and areas of our lives.

In our first volume, *The Courtship of God...A Journey of Love and Transformation,* we share the story of how the Divine Matchmaker put us (Jim and Shelvy) together as a couple; we also explore God's particular wooing of each of us in every season of life, from conception to the time of our earthly departure. We address the various ways we can be wounded in early years, but also show how with God, it's never too late to receive the healing we need.

It is God's sacrificial love that causes Him to woo us and choose us as His own. He has lovingly stepped into the circumstances of our lives to evidence Himself as our Protector and Provider, Savior and Deliverer, the Lover of our soul. His love covers a multitude of sins and His love never fails. Receive His love and let it transform you forever. This is the Courtship of God!

We feel it is a sacred trust for people to open their hearts and lives to us when they come for prayer counseling. Therefore we never breach that trust by disclosing information that would identify anyone in our counseling sessions. Still we do tell stories to illustrate the principles in the Word of God, giving testimony of the transforming power of God's love through His Word. While these stories are based on the many cases we've seen, we never use actual names of people or places, and specific personal details are changed. In most instances we combine several cases, removing identifying aspects of their stories. These cases span more than 30 years and over 50,000 hours of counseling time.

It is our prayer that the reader will receive hope and encouragement that no matter what their need or problem, our God is the God of the Impossible and nothing is too difficult for Him, the Wonderful Counselor.

"And they overcame him by the blood of the Lamb and by the word of their testimony, and they did not love their lives to the death." (Revelation 12:11)

1

Betrothal, What Is It?

"Betrothal" is not a word that is used today. To help discover its meaning, let's look at Amos 3:3: *"Do two walk together unless they have agreed to do so?"* The footnote in the New Spirit-Filled Life Bible, reads as follows: "The root word in Hebrew for 'agreed' is to 'fix upon,' and also means 'a summons to a set tribunal at a fixed time and place.' The same word is translated 'to betroth,' indicating a mutual commitment." [1]

So a commitment to marry or a pledge to marry is an agreement between a man and a woman.

We commonly speak of someone being "engaged" to be married. But being betrothed is so much more than that. To look at that "much more," we examine the lives of three young women in the Bible.

But first let us tell you our story—how we became betrothed.

I (Shelvy) was a widow living in Virginia Beach. I had no thoughts of ever marrying again and was quite happy: "Just me and You, Lord." But He had a different idea. On March 27,1985 I woke up from a dream that became very significant in my life. In this dream I saw a man I did not know. He was tall with salt-and-pepper hair and beard. He had on a light blue, V-neck sweater. He was standing with his arms folded across his chest and three or four men were talking to him. There were other people in the dream also. I wrote the dream down in my journal and prayed about it for several days, and then I forgot about it.

---

[1] New Spirit-Filled Life Bible, p.1114 (2014 Thomas Nelson)

About four months later, I received a phone call from the only person I knew who lived in the state of Connecticut—a woman I had met while on a trip with John and Paula Sandford in the holy lands of Israel. She was coming to visit Regent University in Virginia Beach, and would be traveling with two friends from her church. I invited to take all of them to dinner. When I met the man in her party, I thought he looked very familiar. But I had never been to Connecticut, and it did not appear that we had ever met. Some time later, she and I were walking up the aisle in church and when I looked up, there he stood. Jim Wyatt was wearing a light blue v-neck sweater and three or four men standing in front of him were talking. I got cold chills as I realized he was the man in my dream from four months earlier. I knew God was up to something. (For the more complete story of our meeting, read our first book, *The Courtship of God, A Journey of Love and Transformation*.)

The Lord was doing so many things that we couldn't just call them coincidences. God brought us together for His purposes. While attending a Sandford Conference in Connecticut, John asked Jim and me to minister together. We were both amazed at how the Spirit led us as we prayed for people. I was attracted to the godliness I saw in Jim.

Jim tells his perspective:

I had been divorced for ten years. I had come to know the Lord in a profound way and was repentant of having walked away from my marriage. It took five years for me to approach my former wife with the idea of reconciliation; she was not interested for she had met someone else. I was willing to be married again, but I knew it had to be God's doings.

When I met Shelvy, God was doing something in both of our hearts and we were committed to His will, whatever that was. After three months, several visits and multiple phone calls, I asked Shelvy to marry me.

Back to Shelvy:

Once we both agreed to be married, we called it a betrothal and not an engagement because we knew this was God's plan from beginning to finish. Now we wondered *when* we were supposed to get married; God was planning everything else.

We had each been to Israel several times and loved the holy lands. We thought it would be a great place for a honeymoon—or even for the marriage ceremony itself. Jim called John to find out what their schedule looked like. He and Paula were leading a tour group in Israel in March 1986; he said he could marry us on the morning of the twenty-seventh at the church on the Mount of Transfiguration. When Jim told me, I couldn't believe what I was hearing. I said to Jim, "Do you realize what March 27 is?"

"It's Thursday before Easter," he replied.

Through tears I said, "March 27 was the date of the dream where I first saw you!"

God does all things well!

Mary

Mary was betrothed to Joseph; if they did not follow through and get married, not only would they be in disobedience to the pledge they made before God to one another, but it would require Joseph to give Mary a certificate of divorce. That's how deep the commitment is with betrothal.

When Mary was betrothed to Joseph, she was promised or pledged to him. They were not yet married, but everyone knew she was to be his bride. When he had everything ready, including a home of their own, he would come for her and make her his new bride.

In the meantime, she prepared herself for that special day, her wedding day, when she would begin her new life as Joseph's wife.

But before that day came, she had a visitation from the angel Gabriel. He told her that the Holy Spirit would come upon her and she would be with child. She responded, "How can this be since I am a virgin? He told her that the Holy One to be born would be the Son of God and He was to be named Jesus.

Now put yourself in Joseph's shoes upon hearing this news. What should Joseph do? Should he give her a certificate of divorce? That is what it would take to dissolve the pledge to get married. It looked like she had been unfaithful to him. Being a godly man, he didn't want to expose her to the public, so he thought he would put her away quietly and hand her a certificate of divorce. He must have been brokenhearted.

That night he had a dream; he was told to take Mary as his wife but not consummate the marriage until after the birth of the child, because the child was conceived by the Holy Spirit of God. (See Matthew 1:18 ff or Luke 1:26 ff for the full story.)

How God Betroths

There are only two books in the Bible named after women: Ruth and Esther. Both books tell beautiful love stories. In both cases, God arranged the circumstances of their lives to betroth them to the husband of His choice. In one book a Gentile marries a Hebrew and in the other, a Hebrew marries a Gentile.

Ruth

The book of Ruth begins with famine and death, but it ends with love and fruitfulness. In the first chapter we read a familiar passage of Scripture that we have heard read at many weddings. It is Ruth speaking to her mother-in-law, Naomi. *"Entreat me not to leave you, or to turn back from following after you; for wherever you go, I will go; and where you lodge, I will lodge; your people shall be my people, and your God, my God." (1:16)*

Ruth was going about her daily work, not knowing that her future husband was observing her as she labored in his fields. Boaz, a wealthy Jewish man owned the fields and made inquires about who she was. Her reputation went before her as he was told of her dedication to her mother-in-law after the death of her own husband. She'd left her own country and had come to a land she did not know. It was reported to him that she'd come asking permission to glean in his fields and had worked since early morning. When Boaz spoke with Ruth, he invited her to stay in his fields and not go anywhere else, assuring her that he had commanded his men to not touch her. Then he offered her water, and at mealtime he gave her bread. He also instructed his men to leave extra bundles of barley in the field so she wouldn't have to work so hard. Boaz demonstrated his interest in her by being her protector and provider.

Then it was her turn to let Boaz know that she was interested in him. Naomi told Ruth that Boaz was a near-kinsman and therefore, could redeem her and the land of her family. Ruth would be included in this redemption. Naomi instructed Ruth on how she was to prepare herself to go to Boaz. It was harvest time, and Boaz would eat, drink and sleep at the threshing floor. Ruth waited until he was asleep, then went to him, uncovered his feet and lay down at his feet.

When he found her there, he asked, "Who are you?"

She answered, *"I am Ruth. Take your maidservant under your wing, for you are a close relative." (See Ruth 3:4–9)*

Boaz knew what that meant; she was offering herself to be his bride, to come under his authority. It sounded like he was overjoyed: *"Blessed are you of the Lord, my daughter! For you have shown more kindness at the end than at the beginning, in that you did not go after young men, whether poor or rich. And now, my daughter, do not fear. I will do for you all that you request, for all the people of my town know that you are a virtuous woman."* Again he looked out for Ruth's reputation by instructing the men to not let it be known that she came there at night. Next, Boaz did what he always did when he was with Ruth; he gave to her. He said to her, *"Bring your shawl"* and he filled it with barley. His generous heart of love overflowed whenever he was around her.

God betrothed Ruth to Boaz without either of them knowing of His plan. It was carried out by their obedience to His leadership each step of the way. This illustration is one of the many diverse ways God brings two together to become one.

Esther

The book of Esther has the distinction of not having any mention of the name of God, yet we find His fingerprints all through it. Esther was a young Jewish girl and the scriptures say she was lovely and beautiful. She was orphaned and lived with Mordecai. She was his uncle's daughter. When the king commanded that young women be gathered and brought to the palace, Esther was among them. Mordecai instructed her to not reveal that she was a Jew. She entered into a time of twelve months of preparation before she would be called on to meet the king, who was searching for a new queen. The scriptures record that Esther *"obtained favor in the sight of all who saw her." (2:15)*

When the time came for Esther to meet the king, she must have made quite an impression on him. *"The king loved Esther more than all the other women, and she obtained grace and favor in his sight more than all the virgins; so he set the royal crown upon her head and made her queen."* (2:17)

As the story unfolds, a man named Haman has been promoted to an important position of power under the king, and he has set out to destroy all the Jews. When Mordecai learned of the order *"to annihilate all the Jews, both young and old, little children and women in one day,"* (3:13) he sent word to Esther. He instructed her to go to the king and plead for the people.

Her response to him: *"All the king's servants and the people of the king's provinces know that any man or woman who goes into the inner court to the king, who has not been called, he has but one law: put all to death, except the one to whom the king holds out the golden scepter, that he may live."* (4:11)

Mordecai sent word back to her: *"You're going to die anyway. If you keep silent, you may miss the opportunity and the purpose for your being where you are in the king's life. Who knows whether you have come to the kingdom for such a time as this?"* (4:14)

It isn't by chance that God betrothed Esther to the king long before either one of them knew about it. He knew that beneath her beauty was the strength and character to carry out His purpose for her being queen. His plan was to take a young Jewish orphan girl to save the whole nation of Jews.

"For I know the thoughts that I think toward you," declares the Lord, *"thoughts of peace and not of evil, to give you a future and a hope. Then you will call upon Me and go and pray to Me, and I will listen to you. You will seek Me and find me when you search for Me with all your heart."* (Jeremiah 29:11–13)

Esther sent word to Mordecai to gather all the Jews that he could and fast for her for three days while she and her maids did the same. *"If I perish, I perish!"* (4:16) She was willing to lay down her life to save her people. What holy boldness! She put on her royal robes and went to approach the king.

When the king saw her, *"she found favor."* He held out to Esther the golden scepter that was in his hand. *"What do you wish, Queen Esther? What is your request? It shall be given to you, up to half the kingdom!"*

(5:2) Was she trusting in his love for her? Was she willing to risk her life because she knew the heart of the king, that he would not harm her?

When all those young women were gathered as potential brides for the king, it wasn't by accident that Esther was included. God had a plan long before she knew anything about it. He betrothed her to the king, and He was building in her the character and inner strength to carry out His will and save the whole nation of Jews. He made her lovely, but we believe that the king was attracted to more than what he could see on the outside. She wasn't just another pretty face. Her love for God was even stronger than love for her own life. *Love never fails.*

Lady-in-Waiting

We know a young woman who is preparing to be a bride. She is spending time in prayer and fasting. She is practicing listening prayer and journaling what she hears from the Lord. She is also recording her dreams and asking the Lord to interpret and confirm each dream through His Word. She studies the scriptures daily and is maturing in the Lord as she spends time in the secret place of intimacy in the Lord's presence. What a joy to watch her move from knowing who she is in the Lord to *living* who she is in the Lord. Worship music fills her listening, and she spends time singing to the Lord. She is in love with her Lord and Savior, Jesus Christ.

While young people today stay in touch with friends through the various social media networks like facebook, she closed her facebook account and changed her cell phone number to close the door on all former dating relationships. She has turned down all offers for dating. She knows that she is a lady-in-waiting. She has set her goal to be pleasing to the Lord and being obedient to Him.

We've observed that she takes care of herself; she watches what she eats, wanting to be healthy when her special day comes. She works out faithfully in the gym several times a week so that she will be pleasing in the eyes of the one with whom she is preparing to spend the rest of her life in holy matrimony. The latest fashions are not a concern to her as she seeks what she thinks might look attractive and gracious on her as a woman of God. What would make him proud to have her on his arm?

Before she goes to sleep at night, she kneels by her bed to pray for his protection—body, soul, and spirit. She prays for him to be strengthened in the Lord, to be the kind of leader in their home that would be pleasing to the Lord. She asks the Lord to prepare his heart to receive her as his bride.

She feels that the Lord has betrothed her and she prays that the day will be soon for she has not yet met her husband-to-be.

Interview with the Lady-in-Waiting

There are many who are waiting. So we interviewed this lady-in-waiting, and we think the questions and her answers may be helpful:

- Do you believe Father God has betrothed you to be married?
  YES
- Has He introduced you to His Son, Jesus Christ?
  YES
- Do you believe that He is preparing a husband for you?
  YES
- Do you believe He will arrange for you to meet that man?
  YES
- Do you have certain desires as to what you want in a mate?
  Oh, YES! Most definitely!
- What are some of those characteristics?
  First, he would have to have a huge heart for the Lord. Fully live to what love is, have strength, integrity, lead, not be afraid to speak truthfully to me, listen. I want him to approach God with me in prayer and worship. I want him to know deep within himself from the least to the greatest thing we could ever do, that I am with him and for him, arm in arm. Know that I believe in him. His heart is what matters to me!
- Do you believe that as you live your life to be pleasing to the Lord, you will be prepared for your lifetime mate?
  YES
- How does it help to think of yourself as already betrothed?
  It changes everything: dress, speak, way you go about everyday, being the best you can be.

- Do you think you need to help God by dating a number of young men and being at places where you can meet someone?
  NO! NO! NO!
- Do you think God will bring your future husband into the circumstances of your life in His time and in His way?
  Absolutely YES, without a doubt!
- What has been the most difficult part of this process?
  Once I believed the promise, it became the greatest thing I want. I know God's time is perfect. I once read a quote that said, "When all is said and done, waiting is worship."

We asked our Lady-in-Waiting to write in her own words what this time has been for her:

"There is a word that has too often been made to be complex, when it is simple and it's the word called **waiting.** I have been asked by the God of heaven and earth to do this very thing. And I can honestly say it has marked my journey with wonder and amazement, and more beauty than I ever could have imagined. You might ask how this is possible, especially when it's been several years now, but I can say today that I am more excited and eager to wait than I was yesterday.

The Lord brought a deep conviction to my heart during this time that there was no turning back. It took some time to truly grasp and then believe, but in His faithfulness and love, He helped me. He asked me to not just wait, but to wait with Him. I have never had to wait for anything before, but this was a paradigm shift in the making.

As I began waiting on this promise from God, He showed me the beauty of what it is to be with Him. The more of Him I found, the more I pursued.

There is not a day that has gone by in these past years that I have not learned something about Him as well as myself. The reason for this is, when you are waiting, all you can do is trust God for the things you can't see. He teaches you about those things because they are the things of Him and at the same time He draws from within you the things that are necessary for what you are waiting for.

It's fiery and it's fierce. It's a risk that not everyone will take because you have to relinquish all control to Him. It's a daily death, a letting go of what you want, but in it you fully receive Him. There were many days I did not know how to let go and failed, but there are many more days that I have seen His glory. God is faithful to wait on you in this process. He is faithful to wait on you every moment. And sometimes, you just have to take a deep breath and understand you are still human. There is an unbelievable amount of grace in waiting.

I will say this with full assurance: When you honor God, He honors you. There have been many days I have asked, "How can this be?" And in every moment of doubt He has come in triumphantly to reveal that He holds this promise He made to me in His hands. He has never failed me, so how could I fail Him, no matter how hard it may be? When you choose His ways, He calls it honor.

Waiting is not the way of the world, but it is the way of God. In it, you find immeasurably more than you could ever ask or imagine because when you wait, you give God all the room to be God! I would wait forever if He asked me, for I have seen Him each day because this completely belongs to Him.

If you are waiting, know that you are not alone and although this is the road less traveled, it is the one where Jesus comes to shine. In His shining, you come to see a little more. I have had the privilege to experience the heart of God in ways I cannot begin to describe right now, but they are things that have made me who I am and cause me to believe in who I will become.

So I say, **embrace the waiting**."

Making Ourselves Ready

Just as this young woman is preparing to be a bride, so it is for us as believers. We are betrothed to the King and we must make ourselves ready.

In his insightful book, *Secrets of the Secret Place*, Bob Sorge writes: "We are the bride of Christ, being prepared for a great wedding celebration in the age to come, when we will be joined forever in great affection to our Bridegroom, the Lord Jesus Christ.

"Believers fulfill the feminine role in the relationship as we commune with the Lord. He initiates, we respond; He gives, we receive; He impregnates, we bring to birth; He leads, we follow; He loves, we reciprocate; He rules, we reign with Him."

Sorge goes on to say, "When Jesus looks at us, clothed in white garments of righteousness, replete with good works, mature in affections, making ourselves ready for our wedding day, His ravished heart soars with delight and desire for His espoused virgin, His bride." [2]

May we keep uppermost in our hearts and minds that we are betrothed to the King! Jesus is preparing for the wedding; may we, too, we make ourselves ready in all we do and say. May we be faithful to Him and Him only, forsaking all others.

Timothy Keller writes in *Counterfeit Gods*, "The only way to free ourselves from the destructive influence of counterfeit gods is to turn back to the true One. The living God, who revealed himself both at Mount Sinai and on the Cross, is the only Lord who, if you find him, can truly fulfill you, and, if you fail him, can truly forgive you." [3]

The Apostle Paul writes in 2 Corinthians 11:2, *"For I have betrothed you to one husband, that I may present you as a chaste virgin to Christ."*

℘ Prayer

Father God, help me to always remember that I am betrothed to the King. King Jesus is the One who gave His life for me on the Cross. I want my relationship with Him to be pleasing at all times, in all I do and say. I want my conduct to reflect a heart cleansed and a mind focused on Him, forsaking all others. I want to interact with others in such a way that I remember to whom I am betrothed. Let me be so full of His love that others feel His love and acceptance when they are with me. Let me be aglow with His Spirit. Open my eyes that I may see Your hand moving and working in my life. Help me to be ready when He comes for His bride.

In the name of Jesus I pray, Amen.

---

[2] (Oasis House, P.O. Box 522, Grandview, Mo. 64030-0522, Page 185, copyright 2001 by Bob Sorge)

[3] Introduction pg. xxvi, Riverhead Books, Penguin Group, 375 Hudson St., N.Y., N.Y. 10014)

2

Relationships Gone Bad

Relationships can be like having your family *relations* in a *ship*. You know, *relatives*—people you didn't choose to be on board with you. Like the uncle that is too touchy-feely, the gossiping aunts that know everyone's business, the kissing cousins that get too close for comfort, the older sister who's trying to run your life, and then of course the monster-in-laws! Sometimes on our life's journey we encounter rough seas, and at other times the waters are calm and peaceful. But whatever the weather, relationships in our family-of-origin tend to influence our lives the most, whether for good or bad.

Is history repeating itself in your life? Are you finding yourself doing the very things you said you would never do? Do you feel that no one respects your boundaries? Are they always barging into your personal space so that you have no privacy on this ship?

What about that friendship that you thought would last a lifetime? Instead you find yourself with a foghorn that's always pointing out the dangers ahead—the negatives possibilities in life—so you can't hear yourself think…

What about that long-awaited romantic relationship that seems to be dead in the water or stuck, run aground and going nowhere? Or maybe it feels like you have hit an iceberg and may freeze to death, while this ship promises no warmth or comfort…

What about the work place? You were so hopeful when you started this job. You really thought it would be smooth sailing, launching you into a new career. Do you feel like you would like to be at the ship's helm to guide the ship on its way? But instead you are being controlled by someone who thinks he or she is the captain, and you are just a deckhand and have to do what you are told...

What about that person you respected and looked up to, but now he is so impressed with himself that he doesn't even see the torpedo headed straight for the ship? Meanwhile you know it's going down and there will be no survivors...

You had such high hopes when you began this voyage, and you have been on this ship a long time. But you can see the circumstances. The very atmosphere has changed and you are headed for the perfect storm and you know there is no escaping it—you are going to break up. You gave this relationship everything you had—body, soul and spirit—and now it looks like it was all for nothing and you feel like you are worth nothing...

When you signed on this lifetime journey of marriage, you had no idea there was so much baggage on board that the ship was in danger of sinking.

No matter how hard you try to signal that something is wrong, your message doesn't seem to go through. Not only that, but also your ship keeps getting compared to the newer model ships that have so much more appeal. You try to stay "ship shape" but feel used and abused. Time has taken a toll, and now the ship looks battered and the paint is chipped. There have been promises of a new paint job, but you feel nothing will change because underneath it's the same old ship...

There are times when it's too scary to stay on board. The ups and downs are unpredictable and you never know how the wind is blowing. Maybe jumping over board and swimming with the sharks would be better... You can't help but think about seeing one of those shark lawyers about getting a divorce. There doesn't seem to be any other way out...

The people around you communicate with others but not with you. It feels as though the unspoken message is, "If you don't talk about the problems, they'll go away." There aren't enough provisions on board and you are starving to death and you don't just mean food...

Now you find yourself in dry dock—isolated; you have become part of the Moth Ball Fleet. It feels like a big "D" is painted on you. Does it stand for Discouraged, Disappointed, Divorced, Deficiency, Dismal failure, or just plain old Dead? That's the way you feel. Is your final prayer "Rust In Peace?"

All your hopes and dreams turned out to be relationships gone bad!

Do any of these scenes describe your experience? With God, it's not the end of the story…

✆ Prayer

Lord, I come to You with a broken heart. My relationships have not turned out the way I hoped they would. I know I made my share of mistakes; forgive me. Help me to forgive those who have hurt me and disappointed me. Forgive me for looking to others for my happiness instead of looking to You first. Heal my broken heart and give me the grace to try again. As memories of the past come to my mind, help me to let go and trust that You will take care of any unfinished business. Forgive me for not making my relationship with You the most important. Forgive me for neglecting You and not talking to You and not listening to You. Some of my hurtful relationships are because I didn't talk with You about them. Forgive me for not gathering daily manna, reading Your Word, feasting at your table; then I wouldn't have been so hungry that I accepted crumbs from the table of society. Thank You for loving me and never giving up on me. Help me to remember that I am betrothed to the King and let that guide all my relationships. I offer this prayer in the name of Jesus Christ, the King of Kings!

Marriage Interrupted

"We interrupt this program to make a public service announcement." Many a radio or television program has been interrupted to make an announcement of importance. Sometimes it's tragic news, such as a beloved president being shot. Other times, it's to announce that war has been declared. Or a hurricane is just a few miles away and it's time to take cover. In an instant, our lives are changed.

"My husband doesn't love me anymore." Through sobs, this attractive mother of three tells her story. "He wants a divorce." How often have we heard these words, usually followed by, "And he's found someone else." Marriage interrupted. Bad news!

Some marriages are interrupted by illness, accidents and traumas, such as the death of a child, loss of a job, an affair, or addiction. All these things are serious challenges that can put great strain on a marriage. Death and divorce are of course major interruptions to what we thought would last "until the end of time."

Most veterans of marriage have war stories to tell. For some, the battles began on the honeymoon or before. They've seen differences of opinion, arguments, skirmishes, peace talks that went awry; ultimatums and sanctions that sometimes ended in hostile takeovers... "I didn't sign on for this!" many declare.

But then when these veterans are just as quick to tell of the victories—the close calls, the near fatal mishaps, the successful negotiations and truces, peace talks that accomplished peace—you know the war has been won. It's too bad that some concentrate so much on keeping score and winning the battle that they actually lose the war.

Even with victories, every war has its casualties. Only about half who make a lifetime commitment of marriage make it to the finish. The bar stools are lined with those who went AWOL. Singles' chat rooms on the Internet are filled with the lonely, the disenchanted and the battle-weary. Sad to say, not all of those people are single. We have had many come to us wanting to get out of their marriage because they have "met someone on the Internet."

Some proudly show their scars and sound their battle cries. "My wife doesn't understand me!" Then there are those who talk of separation, restraining orders, divorce and alimony. Their lives have been turned upside down. Many numb their inner pain with "one more drink" and other addictions. Their stories are locked up inside, never to be told. But we feel it's important to tell the stories.

We believe that it often helps to share even painful stories, not to focus on the problems but to help people identify what's going on in their lives and begin to turn right side up again.

Stories of healing and hope can encourage people in their healing journeys. God's own love story—good news of His great love for us—is the place to start on this journey. We use this ancient art of storytelling in all our books. Uniquely threaded through each chapter are the testimonies of people we have had the privilege of encouraging through our counseling ministry.

No matter what life struggle we are facing, God's main message to us shows up in His courtship. Have you ever thought about how God courts, woos, and expresses His love? Whether we are married or single, He patiently pursues us like no other. We marvel at how the Lord of all Creation is also a very personal Admirer and Lover of our souls. His love is far greater than romance, as wonderful as that is. Our deep desire to be fully known, valued, understood and affirmed can be answered by God better than any other; after all, He's the one who created that desire in us. He's also willing to wait until we're ready to receive more fully from Him. God loves us unconditionally regardless of our ability to respond to Him, and He plants clues for us all through our lives, for that time when we can finally begin to recognize them as the love notes that they are.

When It Gets Worse

When we say our wedding vows "for better or for worse," we don't really think about the worst ever happening. We are usually quite optimistic and very much in love. But then we come back from the honeymoon and life happens.

A husband returns home from military service and is suffering from Post Traumatic Syndrome after active duty in a war zone. He doesn't seem like the same man who stood at the altar, saying, "I do." What's a wife to do? She understands a little of what he has been through, but his mood swings from depression to anger are difficult to live with. How can she honor her husband and still protect herself and their children from his violence? Can God give her the grace to continue to love him? Is it true that love never fails? Will God give her the wisdom to know what to do?

What about the couple who desperately wants a child but hasn't been able to conceive? Does God really want them to have an "empty nest"? Can they trust Him to give them a child, through adoption, perhaps? They find that the peace comes when they stop blaming each other and put their eyes on Him, the Giver of all life…

What about the long awaited son who is diagnosed with autism? Is God punishing them? Does God have a purpose for his life? How can they love him when he stresses them out so? Can their marriage hang together with this major disruption? Will they even be able to take vacations? Who will care for him when they are dead and gone?

What about the couple that met and fell in love in college, married after graduation, raised children, went through ups and downs in a career, celebrated 50 years of marriage…and then one spouse begins to forget more than she remembers? "Alzheimer's"—the dreaded diagnosis—begins to rob this couple as, little by little, she doesn't even remember who he is. He must stand by and watch while the woman he loves changes into a stranger and he is left alone to grieve the losses of the life they shared and the dreams for the future. Yes, he said, "until death do us part"—but must it be this *living death*? He said to us, "So much pain and sorrow! Where is God? Can this really be happening to us? Why God, why?" For better or worse—this is the worst!

What to do when the job is lost? Will we lose the house? Who am I if I don't have a career? What am I worth when I can't support my family?

What about the spouse who finds out an affair has been going on? What to do? Why doesn't he love me anymore? Why wasn't I enough?

What about the auto accident that leaves one spouse in a wheelchair? How can we survive under these circumstances?

On and on the questions come, as lives are hit with one interruption after another. Maybe each unexpected and unwanted event is an opportunity for God to manifest Himself—a time for us to find out how big our God is and how much He loves us.

When God Intervenes

Let us share with you how God stepped in and turned the "worst" into "better" in a few of the above stories:

♦ The wife of the man with PTSD, anger and violence issues: Her grandmother died and left her a little bit of money. She bought her husband a lifetime membership at a gym. She thought perhaps he could work out some of his aggression. At the gym he met another former military guy and the two of them hit it off. After a while, the guy shared about how the support group he attended at the VA Hospital had really helped him. He invited the man to give it a try. He did and it has helped. She is seeing a difference in her husband and she credits the Lord with divinely intervening.

♦ The couple who so desperately wanted a child but could not conceive: They decided to take Foster Parenting classes. They requested "only infants" and fell in love with the first baby they cared for. When the parental rights of the mother were terminated and they were not able to locate the father, this couple put in papers to adopt the child. That isn't the end of the story. They shared how when they took the baby out for a stroll, it was a little bit embarrassing because the wife was then quite pregnant. We rejoice over the goodness of the Lord.

♦ The elderly couple who were living apart because the wife had Alzheimer's: They found a way to be together. When the husband sold the home they had lived in for 40 years, their daughter and her husband came and made a suggestion. They were willing to build an "in-law apartment" onto their house if they could get some help with the finances. The elderly couple now live in that apartment and have a Home Health Aid that comes daily to help care for the wife. He feels so much better being with the woman he has loved all his adult life. God makes a way when there is no way.

♦ The man who lost his job: Two days before he worked his last day, he received a phone call that changed his life. Years earlier he'd applied for what he felt was a better job than what he had, but he hadn't gotten that job at the time. However, the Lord hadn't finished with him yet. The man who interviewed him earlier called and said the man they hired had not worked out. If he was still interested, they would love to talk to him. God's Word says, *"A man's gifts make room for him and bring him before great men." (Proverbs 18:16)*

We need to remember that in every circumstance, our God is the God of the impossible and nothing is too difficult for Him. He specializes in relationship, so as you take all your concerns to the Lord, remember that He has betrothed you to Himself; He cares and He loves to answer your prayers.

A Higher Motivation

They stood at our door and looked nervous, as many are when they come for their first counseling session. In their thirties, they had been married for more than a decade. When their story unfolded, it was a familiar one. She was devastated that her high school sweetheart, husband, father of her children had betrayed her. As she told of his infidelity, the tears flowed and the lines of pain deepened on her brow. Should she just divorce him and be done with it? Could she ever trust him again?

He responded by compartmentalizing: "It didn't mean a thing. It just happened."

Her question to him was barely audible; through sobs we heard her ask, "But do you love her?"

He replied immediately, "No, I don't love her. I love *you!*"

Before the evening was over, he traded the religion of his childhood for a personal, love relationship with the living God through Jesus Christ.

> *They both made a commitment to work on their marriage: he, building a new track record of trust and she, learning to walk by faith rather than fear. Thus began their journey with the Wonderful Counselor.*

But that isn't the end of the story. A few years later, we saw them again. The precious wife was fearful that the same circumstances were presenting themselves that had led to the adultery the first time. They were both working a lot of hours and busy with the children's activities. They had been neglecting quality time together. She said their intimacy had "gone out the window," their date night had fallen by the wayside. They had become like two ships passing in the night. She sat up a little taller this time and boldly asked her husband, "Have you been unfaithful again?"

Without a moment's hesitation he answered. We were surprised to see this macho guy choke up with tearful emotion as he said, "I wouldn't do that to the Lord, not after all He's done for me."

What a glorious answer! There was no doubt in our minds or the mind of his wife that he was telling the truth. He had a higher motivation than being faithful to his wife, as important as that is. He wanted to be faithful to his Lord.

The apostle Paul said in 2 Corinthians 5:14, *"The love of Christ constrains us."*

Another way of phrasing that verse is, *"It's Christ's love that controls us."* This young husband had truly been transformed by the power of God's love, and that love enabled him not only to remain faithful to his wife, but also to the Lord.

Wives Can Make a Difference—Good or Bad

Let me tell you another story that illustrates what happens when marriage is interrupted. We have had the privilege of being a part of a young man's life for a number of years. We've seen him struggle with alcoholism and then maintain sobriety for almost a decade. He has helped many men come to the same place of healing and freedom. We've seen him learn new ways to function well with what would be a severe handicap for others with the same learning disability.

Jim's mentoring has led him to a saving knowledge of Jesus Christ. He has become a ferocious reader of every book Jim has recommended. Studying the Word of God and praying daily has caused him to grow into a healthy, godly man. All who know him have seen the changes in his life.

He has been blessed with a successful career that has earned him a good salary for many years. He has given to the work of the Lord and helped others financially.

The corporation he worked for, like many others, suffered from the downturn of the U.S. economy. As the company tightened its corporate belt, this man was laid off along with several other employees.

We prayed with him, assuring him that we believed in him. Just as he had been successful in the past, he would be again.

However, this man's wife must have taken lessons from Job's wife. Instead of affirming her husband and encouraging him, she gave in to her own fears and insecurities. She let him know that she saw him as a failure. She had her eyes on the world's systems and soaring unemployment figures.

He stayed at peace and ministered to her with love and compassion. Knowing the laws of God, that you reap what you sow, he has continued to live by God's promises to supply every need, and has comfort in God's Presence in his life. He is growing in his relationship with Christ. We know it is just a matter of time before he will be bringing in a good income again.

In the meantime he has gone out of his way to do thoughtful things for his wife such as preparing a special dinner, taking her out on dates and spending quality time with her. His acts of kindness have gotten through to her; she no longer speaks negatively to him. She sees him networking and obtaining other work through freelancing and consulting. This husband is an example of how one spouse's focus on his own relationship with the Lord can greatly influence the whole marriage relationship. As this husband kept steering for God and didn't give up, eventually the whole ship aligned to head in the direction of His love.

When a Promotion Becomes a Demotion

They were a thirty-something couple with one child. He was a hard worker, she a stay-at-home mom. His hard work paid off when he was given a big promotion. But the promotion meant relocating to another state, and his wife was dead-set against moving. Too attached to her parents, she had never lived very far from them—always in the same town. She refused to move and would not be separated from her parents.

In other words, she chose her father and mother over her husband. He tried to explain to her that if he did not take the promotion he would not have much of a future with his employer. He was right and before long he felt he had to change jobs.

The last time we saw them, he was being eaten up with resentment and bitterness. She devoted her life to her child and her parents and he felt very much left out. After a couple years, he left and filed for a divorce.

This is why the Lord exhorts us to leave father and mother, cleave to one another and become one flesh. (See Genesis 2:24.) When we get married, our priorities change and our spouse becomes number one in our life.

Should She Believe Him?

The two who sat before us were successful by the world's standards. He was in his early forties, very good-looking and personable. He earned a good salary, drove the latest model among the luxury class cars, dressed impeccably and lived in one of the wealthiest communities in the state.

She was attractive, well-groomed, dressed tastefully, but wore a frown on her face. This mother of three had an agenda for our counseling session and it wasn't about the tennis lessons at the country club.

When we ask what they needed counsel for, she jumped in immediately. "Something is very wrong!" She moved down the sofa, away from her husband and turned to face him. "I want to know how long the affair has been going on."

He looked quite surprised as he said, "What are you talking about?"

She pulled a letter from her purse and began waving it around as she fought to hold back the tears. "I just received this letter and it tells it all." The letter she read out loud stated that her husband was having an affair with his secretary.

He reached for the letter and read it to himself. "I don't know who sent this, but it's all a lie."

As counselors we wondered, *who do we believe?* We asked some questions and left plenty of room for both to elaborate. Out came the typical struggles of couples married more than a decade. He was busy climbing the corporate ladder of success, and she was busy raising the children, maintaining a comfortable home and engaging them in the right social circles.

He sounded sincere as he told her how much he loved and valued her. He admitted he could do better at demonstrating his appreciation for her and was open to our recommendations of his leading the family in regular church attendance and taking his wife on weekly dates.

Before we prayed for them, she turned to her husband and said, "I choose to believe you that you have not been unfaithful." She rose from her seat, went over to the wood store and threw the letter into the fire. He met her as she was returning to the sofa, gathered her in his arms and told her she would not be sorry for believing him.

As the months went by, she saw Shelvy a few times as she struggled with doubts. But she also reported that they had not missed a Sunday at church. He took her out on dates and when he was out of town on business, he sent her flowers or other remembrances.

Almost a year had lapsed since we first saw them. The wife called to say she had received a second letter. The letter was dictated by a man who was dying; he wanted his conscience cleared before he met his maker. This is the story that followed: The man worked for the same corporation as her husband. Her husband had received the promotion the man had been hoping for. In addition, her husband's secretary had turned the man down several times when he tried to take her out. His anger fueled his jealousy and he decided to write the letter to get back at both of them.

We rejoiced that the truth had come forth and cleared her husband's name. I affirmed her for making a difficult decision to believe her husband and trust the Lord that she was doing the right thing.

In the Old Testament, Genesis records how Joseph's brothers betrayed him, selling him into slavery where he was thrown in prison for several years. In Joseph's later life he said to those brothers, *"As for you, you meant evil against me, but God meant it for good..."* (Genesis 50:20)

This statement can also apply to this couple: What that man meant for evil, God meant for good. Their marriage is far stronger today than it was before receiving the first letter.

Our experience has been that when the hurt or betrayed person can forgive, God steps in and brings out into the light what had been going on in the darkness. Simply put, forgiveness is this: *Let go and let God.* When we choose to turn over to God the hurts and disappointments, He says, "*Vengeance is Mine, I will repay.*" *(Romans 12:19)*

℘ Prayer

Dear God, when interruptions come, help me to see You "high and lifted up" and "able to work all things together for good." Give me Your wisdom to know what You would have me do when those interruptions come. Help me remember that when it looks like a problem, let me see it as an opportunity for You to manifest Yourself. Thank You for being attentive to my prayers and ever faithful to answer them. I love you, my Lord. Amen

3

Matched Set of Woundings

God is a just God! He never puts a totally messed-up person with a totally whole person. We are *all* wounded in some way. There is usually the obvious one who is acting out, coupled with the one who has a need to be needed or has a need to be right. There are lesser and greater degrees for both, but they will always have a matched set of woundings. All the hurts and lies people have believed about themselves (and about life in general) tend to manifest in their day-to-day living. After more than 50,000 hours of counseling, we have seen this to be true, time and time again. If a wife sees only what her husband is doing wrong and is unwilling to examine her own heart, she will never get to her root wounding. And that pattern will repeat again and again, no matter whom she marries. The one who is the victim always has a hard time seeing that there is anything in himself or herself that needs to change.

Balance and Counterbalance

When we were children, we liked to play on the seesaw. If our playmate was bigger or weighed more, neither one got much of a ride. That is a picture of what happens when we marry. Opposites really do attract.

- ♦ The EXTROVERT admires the quiet INTROVERT and thinks, "I should be more like that."
- ♦ The INTROVERT wishes she were more outgoing.

- The SPENDER is attracted to the SAVER who always has some money squirreled away.
- The SAVER wishes she had the freedom to buy whatever she wants.
- The LATE mate will complain about the mate who always wants to be early.
- The EARLY mate wishes she were more relaxed and not so anxious about the need to be on time or (even better) a little early.
- The AGGRESSIVE go-getter will be attracted to the calm, passive person.
- The PASSIVE one wishes she had the nerve to speak up more instead of holding back.

(Disregard references to gender; either can play any role.)

When we marry and become one, we then have the power to throw our mate off balance. What is so ironic is that one may look like the good and righteous one while the other one is just not getting with it. But both are acting out of their wounds. None of us had perfectly functional families-of-origin, so a lot of our behaviors are developed early in our lives. Some wounds come from what has been done to us, such as abuse. Other times, it's what we have done to ourselves. Our memories don't even touch reality sometimes, but those mindsets and habits are what we bring into the relationship.

The good news is that the Lord can heal any and every hurt. He can make us whole, so we can be a blessing to our mates and bring out the best in them instead of the worst.

Each mate needs to own his or her personal behavior and take responsibility. Each one needs to ask forgiveness for the wrongs he or she has done. We have a plaque in our living room:

A successful marriage is the union between two great forgivers![1]

May we all become great forgivers.

---

[1] Adapted from a quote by Ruth Bell Graham

Different Suit, Same Man

The couple sitting before us looked like a mismatch—a real Odd Couple as found in the old movie featuring Oscar and Felix. She sat ramrod straight in her designer suit and he slouched on the couch, wearing work clothes. They had married right out of high school. He helped her work through college, and he said that nothing he did pleased her. He worked overtime to buy her the lovely things she wanted, but then she wouldn't go out in public with him to wear them. He didn't know what else to do. She said she had out-grown him and wanted to move on with her life. She only came for counseling because her mother insisted on it. Needless to say, it was a waste of time. She had made up her mind; she was getting a divorce no matter what anyone said.

In a very short period of time, she was back with a new guy. This one had an MBA degree, worked in business and was wearing a three-piece suit. They were in love and her mother insisted they come for pre-marital counseling, which she was giving to them as one of their wedding gifts.

She was raised in a home with both a mother and father, but her mother was dominant and worked as a career woman. Her father was a hard worker and steady provider, but passive at home.

The new guy was raised by a single mom who worked two jobs to support him growing up. When we asked him a question, he would first look to her before he answered. It was obvious that he wanted to please her. We were sure this was a pattern in his life, looking to please the woman. That's what a little boy had to do when he was being raised with a mom.

It looked like she had a second man who would do whatever it took to please her. And as it was in the first marriage as well as the home where she grew up, clearly he wasn't going to be the leader in the household. We knew this kind of dependency was a breeding ground for trouble.

It was about a year later when she came by herself for counseling. She was pregnant, still working and very tired of "carrying the load" as she put it. She had to make all the decisions and he was afraid for her to quit work because he wasn't sure he could make it on his own.

This kind a dependency always creates ambivalence and contributes to a love-hate relationship. He will love her but he will also hate her. It's safer and less risky for him to let her lead; he can't fail that way. But he will resent her for her dominance. They had a matched set of wounds—both raised by a dominant mother and an absent or passive father. The result was the same.

Remember what we shared about the attraction of opposites and the power to throw each other off balance? It's not unusual to find a super-responsible person married to an irresponsible mate. You get the idea. Now let's look at the great wisdom of God. He can get two healed for the price of one.

Something Is Wrong With Me

This was our first meeting: She sat on the couch and started tearing up as she said, "Something is wrong with me, I keep finding myself in the same fix." She was middle aged and had recently given her life to the Lord in a new way—a more serious way. She had received the Holy Spirit in baptism and had experienced a new joy in living. But at the same time, she felt she was being turned inside out, and she didn't like some of the things she was seeing about her life.

We prayed and invited the Wonderful Counselor to come and reveal what we needed to talk about. What was He doing in her life?

We asked her, "What's going on that made you decide to come for counseling?" She said her husband of almost five years had just lost his second job since they were married. She assured us that he was a hard worker and she knew in time he would have another job, but it was just too much and she felt overwhelmed. "I'm tired of having to be the strong one and hold everything together. Is that asking too much for someone to look after me for a change?"

Her family history revealed that she was the oldest of many children. Her father's work often took him out of town, so he wasn't home as much as she would have liked. She was put in charge of the younger children while her mother worked, sometimes working nights or weekends.

She admitted that in those days she couldn't wait to get away from home and have a life of her own. She married her high school sweetheart, and in their first year of marriage she was pregnant. Her young husband wasn't too happy about that fact. He started coming home late after hanging out with his buddies who were still single. After a few years of marriage and several babies later, she realized her husband had a drinking problem. He lost jobs and was difficult to live with. She had all the responsibility of raising the children in addition to her work outside the home.

When she felt she couldn't take it any more, she heard about Al-Anon from a co-worker. She finally got enough inner strength to say to her husband, "No more. Either get help or get out." He chose the latter and moved out. A divorce followed.

When the last child left the nest, she began to think of a life for herself. She met a wonderful man at work; he was a widower and a little older than she. But that didn't matter to her; he treated her so well.

Her happiness was short-lived. After a couple of years he became ill. She gladly took care of him while she still maintained her job. After about 18 months, he died. She was heartbroken but remembered the old saying, "It's better to have loved and lost, than to have never loved at all."

After about a year, she met her current husband at church. They married and everything was going well until he lost his job as a result of his company's downsizing. He wasn't out of work too long, but here they found themselves in the same situation again. And this is when she began to see this life-long pattern of her having to be the "strong, steady one" in the family.

What was it in her that she found herself in these same situations again and again?

We explained Jeremiah 17:1 to her; the passage says that a message is written on our hearts about life. From the time she was a little girl, the message written on her heart was that she was the responsible one; she had to be there as the caregiver.

Her mother modeled to her a woman who took care of others in need. This pattern had repeated so many times in her life, it was now an expectation written on her heart. The good news is that God came to set her free from that pattern and expectation. The "eyes of her understanding" were opened and she embraced God's truths. She forgave her mother for putting so much responsibility on her. She forgave her father for not being there to affirm and bless her. She forgave herself for the lies she had believed that she wasn't good enough, pretty enough, smart enough, or worthy of a man who would be there for her. She put God on the throne of her heart and chose to believe He was the strong one and He would always be there for her. She renounced the "need to be needed" and she accepted the unconditional love of God, something she did not have to work for or earn. He loves her just because she is and not for anything she does or does not do.

As iron sharpens iron, so a man sharpens the countenance of his friend. (Proverbs 27:17)

Marriage is one of the greatest refining tools that God has. Iron sharpens iron...and the sparks fly!

> *There's nothing like marriage to deal with that chip on your shoulder. And if you think you don't have any problems and your life is pretty much together, just get married and you'll find out there are still a few things God wants to refine and purify in you.*

When I became a widow, I thought, "It's just You and me, Lord. You're all I need or want." But the Lord had different ideas. It was as though He was saying, "I still have a lot of work to do on you to get you ready to spend eternity with Me. And the best way to do that is to get you married again."

"No one discovers himself or herself in solitude. It is only by giving of self that one can find oneself."[2]

When Helping Is Not Helping

The couple arrived on time for their first session of marriage counseling. It was downhill from then on. He sat on the couch, and she sat in a chair as far from him as possible. She spoke up first: "I'm not here to work on the marriage. It's over. I just want to make sure my children are provided

---

[2] J. Keith Miller, *More Than Words* (2002 Baker Books)

for." Then the story poured forth from both of them with a lot of blaming back and forth as the volume of their voices went up.

They'd been married about ten years and had four children. He was in a helping profession and had gotten involved with a young lady in need. This young lady called him one time too many, and he responded to her because he thought his wife didn't have time for him. He said her time was consumed with the children and working a part-time job.

The wife said that very often the Lord spoke to her through dreams. She had a dream that this particular young lady was in their marriage bed between her and her husband. She was startled by how real the dream was when she woke up. Her husband saw the look on her face and asked, "What's wrong?"

She told him of the dream and after the shock of it, he denied any involvement. Eventually the truth came out and he confessed that it was true.

The wife had just found out that she was pregnant with their fourth child. She also found out that the girl in her dream was pregnant too, by her husband.

He broke off with the girl but said he would take responsibility for the child financially. The girl called him whenever the baby was sick or with any other excuse she could come up with, or so the wife said. Once a week he went to her apartment to give her money for the child's support.

We knew there needed to be some new boundaries set up for all concerned.

Boundaries

We recommended that the following be held to: He was to have the child-support money sent by his bank. No more personal contact. No more going to the girl's apartment. The girl was to be instructed not to call him as he was committed to his wife and working on restoring his marriage. The couple was *not* to discuss divorce while we worked with them. All discussions on their critical issues were to be done in the counseling sessions and not with each other or family or friends.

They were to plan a family activity once a week. The children needed assurance that their world was secure. They needed to make the home a place of peace. The family was to attend the same church together each week.

At that point we felt we should see them separately and work on each taking responsibility for their own participation for the mess of their marriage. We knew that if we didn't help them get at the root issues, they were destined to repeat their behaviors.

Roots

> *There are Biblical principles that are at work whether we have knowledge of them or not. God's laws are for our benefit, and in keeping them, our lives work better.*

We begin by looking at the fruit in a person's life and then with the help of the Holy Spirit, we go into the root system of his or her individual life, including the family tree. We want to see where a seed was sown that might have produced this destructive fruit.

"*Do not be deceived: God is not mocked; for whatever a man sows, that he will also reap.*" (Galatians 6:7)

It was not surprising to us to find that both were raised by a mom with no father present in their lives. We needed to explain female dependency; we could see those generational patterns repeating.

More patterns were about to repeat if they went through with the divorce. They were both in helping professions, trying to prove their worth by helping others. Because of the lack of fathering, they had not been affirmed and blessed for who they were. So they sought affirmation by performing well. Both needed the healing touch of the Father. We began by searching out their parents' lives and how their lives had affected them. It's interesting to note that the first commandment the Lord gave us with promise attached concerns our parents: "'*Honor your father and mother' which is the first commandment with a promise… 'that it may be well with you and that you may live long on the earth.'*" (Ephesians 6: 2–3; also Exodus 20:12)

What is not going well in your life? Examine the bad fruit and know that somewhere in the past a seed was sown. With the couple we were counseling, it wasn't a coincidence that the marriages of their parents did not go well—and now *their* marriage was not going well.

It only seems natural that as children, people assess the behavior of their parents and decide they were wrong. But when they make inner vows to not be like their parents, they have dishonored their parents through judging. Judging is not the same as discerning the facts or truths in a situation. Judging is simply passing a judgment or sentence on the one judged. For example, "I'll never do *that* in my life!" or, "She did a bad thing and deserves punishment." Sometimes our judging is sub-conscious, forgotten. But just the same, we've decided the case in our hearts. Meanwhile God is the only one who is righteous enough to do that. God is the only one that can look at the heart, and therefore only He can know the complete story.

Which brings up the question: How do you honor parents who have done dishonorable things? As with this couple, both fathers had abandoned their children. Both mothers had to work long hours to financially support their children. The older children had to take care of the younger ones. None of them received the love and attention that they deserved. So, how to honor? Does God really expect that and if so, why? What difference does it make?

"Judge not, that you be not judged. For with what judgment you judge, you will be judged; and with the measure you use, it will be measured back to you." (Matthew 7: 1–2)

We need, first of all, to ask God's forgiveness for our sin. Then we choose to be obedient to God's word and "even as Christ forgave you, so you must also do." (Colossians 3:13b) Now, as an act of our will, we choose to honor our parents in our hearts because God gave us life through them. This does not mean that they will ever acknowledge that they did something wrong. This does not mean that they are safe to be with (if they have been abusive) or that you can have a relationship with them at this time. This is business between you and God.

Empathetic Defilement

The man who had reached out to help a "damsel in distress" had been caught in a web of sin and deceit. We needed to explain empathetic defilement to him.

Empathetic defilement occurs when we are empathizing with

someone. We aren't just listening to his or her words but we are also reading body language. When we go beyond that and listen with our hearts, we are receiving what's in the other person's heart and spirit. If we are in a vulnerable and needy place at the time, it's easy to pick up on where the other person is, identify with it and translate it as being our own thoughts and feelings. In the case of this man, he felt sorry for this young girl and wanted to comfort her.

He reached out to hug her. Meanwhile she was thinking what a wonderful man he was and how it might be if he was *her* man. Lust entered her heart; he picked up on it, not as *her* lust but as *his own*.

He didn't realize that the lustful thoughts originated with her; he translated them as his own and then because he was in a place of need, he wrongly acted on them.

"Pursue peace with all people, and holiness, without which no one will see the Lord: looking carefully lest anyone fall short of the grace of God; lest any root of bitterness springing up cause trouble, and by this many be defiled; lest there be any fornicator..." (Hebrews 12:14–16a)

This man was angry and bitter toward his wife. He felt rejected and neglected, that she had put the needs of the children and her part-time job before him. He felt that since he was "sorry about what happened" with the girl, everything should just go back to the way they were. We can be "sorry" because we got caught or "sorry" for the consequences and not truly repentant at all for the wrong doing and hurt to others. Being "sorry" is ambiguous, whereas asking forgiveness is taking responsibility for our own sinful action.

He needed to see that through judging his wife, he had done the very same thing to God. He had neglected the Lord and no longer had time to spend in His presence, listening for His voice, studying the Word or praying. He had confessed his sin to the Lord and had hoped his wife wouldn't find out about it. After all, (he thought to himself) he was helping a lot of people—didn't that count for something?

Empathetic defilement is a subject that needs to be taught to all those in the helping professions. Unfortunately, we have seen many get involved in wrong ways because they were not aware that another's thoughts were defiling them. God wants us to empathize, but we must keep our hearts clean before Him. We need to pray David's prayer often:

"*Search my heart, O God.*" *(Psalm 139:23)* And we need to pray cleansing prayers for ourselves after helping people: "Come with the cleansing waters of Your Holy Spirit and wash over me, my mind, my emotions, all of me." "*Watch and pray lest you enter into temptation. The spirit indeed is willing, but the flesh is weak.*" *(Matthew 26:41)*

The Process

Working with the couple individually, we first got them to take responsibility for their own responses to what had happened in their marriage. We wouldn't let them talk about what their spouse did or did not do, except to reveal how they acted or reacted to the other's actions.

We asked them to share with us their conversion experience to make sure they knew the Lord personally. This enabled them to see how far they had drifted from their first love. We gave each one a journal and instructed them to spend time with the Lord, writing down their prayers and listening to what the Lord had to say to them. To make sure they did this assignment, we asked them to bring the journal with them on their next session with us. When they got their personal relationship with the Lord back on track, we began to make progress.

She was still sleeping in one of the children's rooms. They had begun to talk civilly about the business of the day—who would pick up the son from ball practice, who could pick up the cleaning from the dry cleaners, etc. As we'd done with others, we had instructed them to not talk about any of their marital problems, but to bring them to the counseling session.

Generational Strongholds

As they began to understand generational strongholds, we examined the family-of-origin history. This helped them to forgive and come to true repentance. They were also motivated because they did not want their children to go through the same mistakes they had made. We explained that the Lord delighted to bring those structures to death. Early in the counseling process, the husband had said, "Maybe it would be easier to start over with someone else rather than try to straighten out the mess."

The Lord opened his eyes to see that that was exactly what his own father had done; it hadn't been easier or solved the problem. He didn't have to repeat that pattern. Meanwhile the wife had said with pride, "My mother raised four children by herself and I can do it too." She, too, saw that she had a choice and didn't have to repeat history.

Forgiveness

We felt it was important to explain what forgiveness is and what it is not. There are many misconceptions about forgiveness:

♦ No, it does not mean the person is getting away with what they did if we forgive them.

♦ No, it does not mean we wait until we *feel* like forgiving.

♦ No, it doesn't mean we pretend it never happened; it isn't forgetting. We remember so we don't repeat the behavior but rather *learn* from it.

♦ Very importantly, forgiveness doesn't mean we have to trust that person again. The offender must restore trust in every instance; that is their responsibility. Trustworthiness is borne out when you see fruit of their repentance in their lives, not by what they promise they will do.

Trust and forgiveness are separate issues.

♦ Forgiveness IS being obedient to God's Word when He says, "*If anyone has a complaint against another; even as Christ forgave you, so you also must do.*" (Colossians 3:13b)

♦ Forgiveness IS letting go of the hurt and offense and turning it over to the Lord. It isn't just blowing it to the wind, but entrusting it into the hands of the One Who loves you. This is business that you do between you and God.

One of our assignments involved forgiveness. "Bring us a list of everyone the Lord reveals to you that you need to forgive." It was encouraging to see that both had put their own names on that list.

When we saw them as a couple, we had them ask forgiveness of each other. "Will you forgive me for_?" (We asked them to be specific.) The spouse was then required to respond. Sometimes that was through tears, to be able to say, "Yes." We were blessed to see healing begin.

Sometimes it's needful to forgive again and again, one memory at a time. It takes a while for the heart to heal. It's a *process*, just as it is a process to believe that the Lord has forgiven us.

Restoring Trust

Now it was the matter of seeing trust restored. Their lives needed to be open books to each other, and that included access to cell phones, computers, etc., being accountable to be where they said they would be and when they said they would be back. We asked them to spend 30 minutes a day talking to each other, heart to heart.

Sometimes face-to-face is too painful to begin with, so we make a few suggestions: Use a notebook, one spouse writes, leaves it in an agreed place and the other spouse responds by writing back. We asked them to respond within 24 hours. When both spouses work, they might want to use email. We ask that they start with facts and then move to their feelings on the subject introduced.

When they have a hard time finding 30 minutes in their day to be together, we remind them that not finding time to open their hearts to one another is what got them in trouble to begin with.

> God made us with the need to connect, to share our hearts. Intimacy is IN-TO-ME-SEE, to be known and loved and accepted for who we are.

Sometimes it's necessary to cut out other time-consuming activities in order to work on marriage. Once some healing had taken place, we asked them to pray together and listen for what God wanted for their future. We wanted them to begin to dream together again. That way they not only experience healing of the old hurts, but can also look forward to something new.

We continue to see this couple as they work on restoring trust and changing some life patterns that will aid in rebuilding their relationship with each other. As they each work to align themselves in their relationship with God, their marriage relationship is destined to flourish.

℘ Prayer

Father God, open my eyes to see all the ways I have passed judgment on the generations before me. Bring to death in me the prideful thoughts that I would never make the mistakes they did. I ask that the Cross of Jesus Christ be placed between me and the generations before me, back through the third and fourth generations. Bring to death in me those un-Christ-like attitudes and habits. I confess that I cannot do any better than those that went before me. It is only Christ in me that gives me hope for a better tomorrow. In Jesus' name, Amen

4.

Affairs: Buying the Lie

"If only I had stayed in my first marriage and tried harder to make it work." As a counselor, I have heard this statement again and again. "This second marriage is so much worse. I feel trapped, like a complete failure!"

Our instant microwave mentality says, "I want it done now!" But when it comes to relationships, we need the slow cooker approach. It takes time to get to know another person, see him in good times and bad. The true character of a person is what comes out in a crisis.

> We have heard it said that marriages are made in heaven, but they come in a kit that takes a lifetime to put together on earth.

That takes time and, I might add, it takes patience, too.

In the counseling office, we hear these statements repeated over and over again (as we have said before, Satan is not creative; he feeds the same lies to whoever will believe them):

"I need to find myself."

"I need space—that's why I'm leaving." (This is when Jim will ask, "What's her name?" ...because there is so often a third party involved.)

"I was too young, I never should have married in the first place."

"I never loved her/him."

"The children will be better off."

"I deserve to be happy."

"It's too late for us – too many problems."

"I love her/him, but I'm not *in* love."

"It will be easier with someone new."

"This new love will satisfy all my emotional and sexual needs."

"I will be happy if I can just get out of this marriage."

"All my problems will be over if I can just get free of my wife/husband."

"I'll do it right the next time."

Although the disgruntled spouse is not always verbalizing these lies in the counseling session with the marriage partner, he or she believes the lies in his heart. In this state of self-deception, the spouse is making as much sense as the teenager who came to us with his mother and said, "I'm sick and tired of my mother always telling me what to do. I'm going to join the Army." This teenager will learn the hard way that he is trading one authority figure for another. But the new authority is an entire Army, and his sergeant won't hold his hand when he's sick or bring him lemonade when he's hot and sweaty. It won't take long in boot camp to find out that the Army's rules are not tempered by love as his mother's are.

Who To Believe?

There are times when we have a couple sitting before us and we don't know who to believe. She says he's having an affair. He says no, he isn't. We're praying silently while they talk: "Lord, reveal the truth and give us the wisdom to know how to help this couple."

He worked as a salesman, spending lots of time traveling. Once a year, his employer would give him a bonus. Each year, they would use the bonus to pay college tuitions—first for their oldest child and then the youngest.

The next time we saw them, he was really angry and down in the dumps. He told us that his boss had just informed him that the company was not doing well and "there will be no bonus this year." He had counted on that bonus to pay for college tuition and he didn't know what he was going to do. He felt betrayed by his boss. "All that hard work for nothing. What's the use?"

His wife blamed him. "He must have done something wrong. Maybe he wasn't working as hard, not paying enough attention to his job. He sure wasn't paying any attention to me. And when he was at home, he wasn't really at home."

Although he tried to blame his wife for not being there for him, he did admit that he had gotten involved with a woman who worked for one of his clients. While we did not excuse his wife's behavior, he was responsible for his own actions. It may sound strange but he was actually relieved to have it all out in the open. He had been under tremendous stress with all the lying and excuses.

We shared with them the biblical principles: The law of sowing and reaping. If you steal, you will be stolen from. By engaging in that extra-marital affair, he had been stealing from his own marriage as well as someone else's. Not only was he taking what was not his to take—the other woman's time, attention and affections—he was also not giving loving attention to his own wife. It wasn't by chance that he didn't receive his usual bonus. He was reaping what he had sown. God was evidencing Himself in the man's circumstances.

We are happy to report that they were willing to do the hard work of restoring their relationship. Below are some of our suggestions for the husband. (Note: These suggestions can easily be adapted and implemented by the wife if the circumstances are reversed, with an emphasis on the husband's need to be respected where you see the suggestions on showing love to the wife. As we've emphasized throughout this book, the main thing is to work at restoration from *both ends* of the relationship.)

FORGIVENESS:
- Ask God to forgive you of your sin (be specific).
- Ask your wife to forgive you for how you have sinned against her.
- Ask the Lord to sever your spirit from that of the other woman.
- Choose to forgive yourself, then ask for cleansing and infilling of the Spirit.

ACCOUNTABILITY (to a friend, pastor, or counselor)

RESTORING TRUST:
- Cut all communications with the other woman, changing phone number if necessary as well as email account.

- Give your wife the password to your phones, computer, etc.
- Give your wife your itinerary and allow her to check on you when you are away; it will prove to her that she can trust you.

REBUILDING RELATIONSHIP WITH WIFE:
- Find out what makes her feel loved.
- Express love and commitment in her love language.

DATES:
- Ask her to go out with you; find out what she would like to do.

COMUNICATION:
- Turn off the TV when she is trying to talk to you.
- Call her to find out how she is doing and let her know you are thinking about her.

Following suggestions such as these, the husband will be taking action to heal his marriage; by his willingness to address his own issues, he's also making more room for God to act on his behalf.

One Mistake Leads To Another

It was the spring of the year, and he was restless; too much time on his hands. He had taken leave, and maybe that was a mistake. He stepped out onto his terrace and saw a beautiful woman bathing. He didn't look away but lusted after her. He made inquiries to find out who she was. She was married, but her husband was off in the war. He sent for her, slept with her and then she went back home. It wasn't long before she sent word to him that she was pregnant.

You have probably guessed by now that we're talking about King David. Yes, the same man who was after God's own heart. (Aren't you glad that the Lord doesn't only tell the *success* stories in the Bible?)

A very human David made one mistake after another. It was bad enough that he committed adultery with Bathsheba, but he compounded that sin with another. He sent for her husband Uriah, and figured he'd get him home and sleeping with his wife so it would look like the child she'd conceived was by her husband. But David didn't know what an honorable man Uriah was. Uriah didn't go home but rather slept at the entrance to the palace with all his master's servants. When it was reported to David what Uriah had done, David sent for him and questioned him. Uriah explained that all the fighting men were camped in open fields; he couldn't go to the comforts of home, knowing that.

David just kept making one bad decision after another. He sent orders that Uriah was to be put on the front lines of the battle where he would surely be killed. And he was.

After a time of mourning, David took Bathsheba as his wife and she bore him a son. As you might guess, things did not go well after that. The child died.

But the Lord wasn't finished with David. He wanted to bring him to true repentance. The Lord sent the prophet Nathan to David and told the story of a rich man and a poor man. The rich man had a large number of sheep and the poor man had one little ewe lamb. When a traveler came to the rich man, he did not take one of his own sheep to prepare for the traveler. Instead, he took the one ewe lamb belonging to the poor man and prepared *that* for dinner. David became angry when he heard this story and said that the rich man deserved to die. At that point, Nathan said to David, "You are the man!" David's response was, "I have sinned against the Lord." (For the complete story read 2 Samuel 11 & 12.)

Our sins will always find us out.

But our God is a merciful God. As David repented of his sins, he was restored. God blessed the union of David and Bathsheba and gave them a son who would become great—a man of wisdom: Solomon.

As recorded in 1 Kings 3, Solomon asked the Lord for wisdom; some translations read, "hearing heart," "discerning heart" or "understanding mind."

"Now, O Lord my God, You have made Your servant king instead of my father David, but I am a little child; I do not know how to go out or come in. Your servant is in the midst of Your people whom You have chosen, a great people, too numerous to be numbered or counted. Therefore give to Your servant an understanding heart to judge Your people, that I may discern between good and evil. For who is able to judge this great people of yours?" (1 Kings 3:7–9)

Notice the humility of Solomon, a grown man referring to himself as "a little child" and needing God's wisdom to carry out his responsibilities as King.

The Lord responded to Solomon's request as recorded in verses 10–14: *"The speech pleased the Lord, that Solomon had asked this thing. Then God said to him: 'Because you have asked this thing, and have not asked for long life for yourself, nor have asked riches for yourself, nor have asked the life of your enemies, but have asked for yourself understanding to discern justice, behold, I have done according to your words; see, I have given you a wise and understanding heart, so that there has not been anyone like you before you, nor shall any like you arise after you. And I have also given you what you have not asked: both riches and honor, so that there shall not be anyone like you among the kings all your days. So if you walk in My ways, to keep My statutes and My commandments, as your father David walked, then I will lengthen your days.'"*

It didn't end there. Verse 15 reads, *"Then Solomon awoke, and indeed it had been a dream."* A DREAM! Can you believe it? All this discourse took place in a dream. And we know that everything God said came true! Better start paying attention to your dreams.

> *Even though Solomon's father David made one mistake after another, his heartfelt repentance opened the way for God to show Himself as Redeemer in his situation. God's blessing of Solomon was very great indeed.*

Emotional Affairs

Many emotional attachments begin in the work place. When we are with someone of the opposite sex for eight hours a day, five days a week, a wonderful working relationship can develop. But if a spouse is not relating in a healthy way at home, it's easy to look to someone who is familiar and is available. Sometimes a co-worker may give words of encouragement and appreciation that aren't being spoken at home.

This kind of atmosphere sets the stage for you to open your heart and share your feelings with another. That's when emotional affairs of the mind can give birth to emotional adultery. If things are not made right in the marriage, it's not a far stretch to cross the line over into the physical.

One man told us that while he worked in the corporate world, his secretary was more than efficient; she had become an important part of his day. She anticipated his needs, bringing him coffee the way he liked it. Whereas at home, his wife was busy with the children even though they were teens. He had to get things for himself. In addition, she was unavailable to him emotionally because her mother lived with them and had become her confidante. His wife had nothing to share by the time he arrived at home.

The secretary was married to a very ambitious man who didn't really have time for her. One day at a low point in her life, she opened up to share her hurts with her boss. In time, the comforting words of the boss led to hugs... then kissing, then the bed.

It may sound strange to say, but he had always been a "man of integrity" and couldn't stay in the marriage while the affair was going on. He left home and filed for divorce. The secretary stayed with her husband and they no longer worked together.

As the man explained how he came to search for more meaning in his life apart from his career, he came into a personal love relationship with Jesus Christ. The Lord began to deal with him about his sin, the affair and how he had hurt his former wife. He sought reconciliation out of obedience to the Lord but confessed to us he had no feelings for his former wife. She informed him that she had met someone else and was marrying that man.

Whenever we open our heart to another instead of our spouse and begin to share our innermost feelings, fears, and dreams with them, we have communicated with "in-to-me-see"—a depth of intimacy that only belongs to our spouse. This is how some emotional affairs begin.

One couple came for counsel because the wife complained that they didn't connect anymore. She said that ever since he enrolled in evening college classes, she never saw him, and he seemed to live in another world that excluded her. He said the classes were important for future advancement with his job.

She said he went to a study group in addition to all the time he was away at classes. He said that since he was older, he needed the help that a study group provided.

When the truth finally came out, it was revealed that he had re-invented himself. He'd claimed to be an unmarried exchange student from Australia and spoke with a heavy accent. He was enjoying all the attention he was receiving as an Australian man—all made up, of course—he'd never been to Australia. He was getting his emotional needs met by the admiration of the young college girls. And all the while, his wife felt emotionally abandoned by her husband.

Truth Revealed

> *God will go to great lengths to reveal truth when we*
> *are open to it.*

One woman came for counsel very worried about her marriage. She'd never really felt bonded to her husband of almost five years. He insisted on keeping separate bank accounts; he would pay certain bills and she would pay others. There were times when he would come to her for funds because he didn't have enough to fulfill his obligations. He became good at dodging questions about how much he got paid and what his over-time pay was. She never knew what time he was coming home from work. He said he just had to stay until the job was done. His secretiveness bothered her, but when she asked questions, he quickly accused her of nagging or being jealous. For almost a year he would fall asleep on the sofa in front of the TV. Once in a while he would get up during the night and come to their bed. He never wanted to go out or do anything to have fun. Needless to say, she too felt emotionally abandoned and left in the dark.

As a counselor, I (Shelvy) suspected that more was going on than what met the eye. I asked if she was willing for God to reveal what was going on—for Him to bring into the light all that was going on in the darkness. I told her she would then be responsible to act on the knowledge that He revealed. There was some fear in her as she shared with me that her family objected to her marrying him and now they would say, "We told you so." But she was miserable and wanted to know what was going on, so she agreed.

Then God gave her a dream: She saw her husband walking with another woman. Their backs were to her but she knew it was her husband. In her dream she thought, "I wish I could see their faces." The woman turned around and she was holding a little baby. The wife woke up with a pounding heart.

When she told her husband about the dream, he just said, "You don't know everything." He walked away and refused to talk about it.

Now she was asking me what to do. Of course, I could not make that decision for her, but I did help her look at her options. I prayed with her that God would give her the inner strength to know and be obedient to His will for her life. It was my view that her husband broke covenant with her, and what she had was not a marriage but a mockery of marriage.

As she continued to seek the Lord for truth, more came out into the light. She found that he had an ongoing relationship with three women through the exchange of inappropriate pictures on his cell phone and computer. After confronting him, she saw that he was not repentant and had no intention of changing, so she requested that he move out. She grieved the loss of the marriage she had hoped to have, and after waiting almost a year she filed for a divorce.

While we can't change others and may have to let them go, God is unchanging in His love for us. He will bring things to light and strengthen us to move on.

so Prayer

Heavenly Father, I come to You with all my hurts and disillusionment. I feel betrayed by the ones I love and trusted. Help me to forgive even when I don't want to. Give me the wisdom to know what to do. Where I have unhealthy attachments to others set me free. Cleanse me of my sinful thoughts and cleanse me of all defilement, both mine and that of others. Forgive me for straying in ways that I know do not please You. Give me hope that I can change and those that have betrayed me also. I am choosing to trust You Lord to straighten out the mess of my life. Thank You for forgiving me and loving me. In Jesus' name, Amen.

5

Caught in the Web: Cyber-relationships

Why do intelligent, sane people get tangled in the Web? Is it dissatisfaction with the life they have? Is it out of loneliness? Is it out of hurt and fear of a flesh and blood relationship? Does it somehow seem safer?

Caught In the Net

Out of loneliness, she sought out former classmates from high school on the Internet. She was in her thirties—attractive, intelligent, and worked out at the gym to stay in shape. She was a wife of 15 years and mother of two children. And she felt lonely because her husband wouldn't talk to her. As she put it, "It's like he uses up his allotted words for the day while he is at work and when he comes home, he has none left—he just wants quiet." When she tried to talk to him, even in their bedroom, his responses would be just "Yes" or "No." He had never been a big talker, but they did used to connect, laugh, and dream together. Over the years, he had put on quite a bit of weight, and she knew he didn't feel good about that. She assured him that it didn't matter to her. She loved him and had never been with another man.

While looking up former classmates, she connected with one in particular, a guy she used to date, if you can call going to school ballgames and dances dating. He lived in another state and she hadn't seen him since graduation. He was also married with children, but things weren't going well in his marriage. Through emails over a period of three months, these two started opening their hearts to one another.

She felt connected with him and felt he wanted to hear what

was going on in her life—every aspect of it. This eventually led to inappropriate intimate sharing.

When her husband went to install some new program on the computer, he found all the emails. Suddenly he wanted a divorce! He didn't want to talk about it, wouldn't speak to her, wouldn't eat anything she prepared for him; in other words, he isolated himself even more than before.

She came for counseling but he would not. My counsel to her was first, to get right with God by **repenting.** She already had; she was broken over her sin. She said, "Looking back, I don't know how I let things go so far." Before coming to see me, she had also gone to her pastor, confessing everything and asking him to pray for her.

I spoke to her of **empathetic defilement.** When she and her high school friend began to open their hearts to one another, they empathized with the predicament each was in with their spouses. Soon, they were feeling what the other was feeling and lust entered, thus defilement.

It was clear to me that she was taking full ownership for her own actions. She wasn't blaming the other guy or her husband.

Next, I counseled her to ask her husband for **forgiveness.** She had already done that too, several times, with no response from him, except to say he was getting a divorce.

"Now, **forgive yourself,**" I said. That was harder for her to do. She said, "I am a Christian, I know better. I spent too much time feeling sorry for myself and I gave up believing that things would ever get any better with my husband. Where do I go from here? I don't want a divorce. I still love my husband and children."

I talked to her about **restoring trust**. Make it clear to your husband that he can check your computer and cell phone at any time. In fact, tell him you want him to check up behind you so he would know you aren't doing anything you shouldn't. Continue to tell him you love him even if you get no response. Make sure your attitude is pleasing to the Lord, everything you do and say *as unto the Lord.*

I told her it sounded like her husband was in depression and was self-medicating with food. We prayed that he would get the treatment he needed.

I assured her that God always has more at stake than anyone. He wants to heal her marriage. She is continuing to humble herself with her husband and trying to keep a good attitude even though it is difficult with his continually saying "I'm getting a divorce." He refuses to allow her to participate in any activities with him and the children. It is under this hardship that she is growing in greater Christlikeness. While her husband hasn't yet been open to working together with her on their marriage, I believe love will win out.

Communication Study

We read of a study on communications by a large university. Their findings were that we communicate 7% with words alone; we add 38% with emotions; and 55% with body language. Therefore when we text or email, we are communicating only 7%. When we call someone on the phone, we can hear the tone of voice and read the emotions, we are now communicating at 45%. It is only when we are face to face with someone that we experience the whole person—his or her body language and spirit—100%. In the light of this information, we have a theory:

> *We would suggest that when we communicate online (especially with someone we don't know well), we're projecting onto those words on the screen an image of what we think that person is like.*

We counseled a young man who had been communicating via email with a young woman in another state for several months. They exchanged pictures and even talked on the phone. When they decided it was time to meet face to face, she flew to meet him. He went to the airport to pick her up, but when he saw her get off the airplane and start walking toward him, he said he knew it was a mistake. He couldn't explain to us how he knew, but he just knew. He made the best of the weekend, but it wasn't the same as it was online.

Is It Love?

A young woman in her mid-twenties told us the following story: Her next-door neighbor introduced her to a middle-aged female relative visiting from another country. The three of them had fun with various activities during the two-week visit. When the woman got ready to return to her homeland, she said she had a nephew the same age as the girl—would she like to meet him via email? The girl said, "Why not?" So she gave the woman her email address.

As she and the young man began to email each other, it did seem that they had a lot in common; soon she could hardly wait to get home from work to check her messages from him. He was so understanding of her feelings and seemed to be everything she'd ever wanted in a man. He was a policeman and enjoyed playing football. He even sent her a football jersey of his with his name on it. She told him she slept in the shirt because it made her feel close to him.

She started saving her money so she could go to see him. Even though he wanted to see her face to face, he seemed reluctant about setting a date for it to happen. He started making excuses: he didn't want her to spend all that money, he wasn't sure he could get time off from work. She persisted and said she'd surprise him if they couldn't come up with a date.

Then the truth came out. There was no policeman who played football. It was the middle-aged woman who had done all the emailing and had made up the fictitious man.

Needless to say, the girl was devastated. She felt betrayed! She was disgusted with herself; she'd thought she was falling in love with a *guy*. She'd opened her heart to him and told him things she had not entrusted to anyone else. She was now able to see how she had projected her own image of her ideal dream man onto the words in those emails.

Can This Marriage Be Saved?

A young man, thirty-something, called from another state to make an appointment for him and his wife to come for counseling. He said he felt the Lord was calling him into the ministry, and his wife had started distancing herself from him. It was several weeks before we could see them.

As it turns out, a lot had happened during those weeks. Between the time of his call to us and this visit, she had left home. He and the two children returned from a church service to find her gone. She left a note saying she had found someone who really loved her and she was going to him.

After the husband had gotten the children to bed for the night, he went into her computer where he found she'd had an ongoing relationship for several months. It was a young man her age who was quite successful. The man had bought a home for his parents as well as a condo on a lake for himself in another state, just a couple of states away from her. He did profess his love for her and his desire to take care of her. At one point, he had given her the phone number at his parents' house because he was going to visit them and wanted to talk with her while he was there.

The young husband decided to call the phone number. An older woman answered the phone and this is the story that came out: The young man was a college student, confined to a wheelchair because of a debilitating disease, and he lived with his parents. His mother apologized on her son's behalf. She said she was discovering that he had several fictitious profiles through which he lived vicariously.

Later that night, this husband received a collect call from his wife. She had left home with little money and no credit cards. She had driven up and down the lake road, had searched the phone book and hadn't been able to locate the young man under the name and address he'd given her. She was several states away and did not have enough money for a hotel, or even to buy gas to drive home. Her husband wired her money as soon as he hung up the phone.

When they came for counseling, she was embarrassed, but also blamed her husband that she had to look elsewhere for a relationship that would meet her needs. He admitted he had been too wrapped up in ministry, and asked her forgiveness. They only came a couple more times, but she was never repentant. A couple of years later they divorced; she had ended up having a real flesh-and-blood affair.

Be Who You Want To Be

One woman came for counseling brokenhearted and disillusioned. She had been married for twenty-plus years, raised three children, all of whom were pretty much on their own by this time. She knew her marriage wasn't perfect, but they had weathered a lot of storms and seemed to come through stronger because of it. Now, she didn't know what to think.

It seemed that she had a luncheon date with her husband and was to meet him at his office. He was in a meeting and his secretary said he wouldn't be a whole lot longer. She decided to go ahead to the restaurant and get a table. She sat at his desk to write him a note to that effect. When she opened his desk drawer to get pen and paper, she found a list of almost two-dozen women's names with email addresses. Beside each name was a man's name, maybe six different names. She didn't know what to think, but she didn't feel good about it.

Her husband was an exciting man to live with. He had given her a number of surprises over the years, some good and some not so good. He was a gambler at heart and had built a business in the stock market. He seemed to have a need for excitement and had a pretty big ego. But she loved him and her faith as a Christian enabled her to accept him unconditionally.

That didn't mean she was going to look the other way; she wanted to find out what was going on. When she confronted him with the information, he made light of it and said it was no big deal. It was a big deal to her, if her husband was communicating with all those women.

He finally confessed that he had developed these six different personas where he could be whoever he wanted to be. It was fun getting to know these women, and living as someone else took him on all kinds of adventures.

He said he had never met any of these women face to face. He assured her that he loved her and was committed to her.

But months later she found out he had gone from the computer to meeting some of the women. She felt he was going through some kind of mid-life crisis, but that is not how a married man conducts himself. He wasn't willing to come for counseling. It wasn't long before he moved out and they did end up divorcing.

> *There are times when it is so hard to forgive. It isn't something we rush into without acknowledging our own feelings and taking responsibility for our own actions and attitudes.*

This precious woman began the hard work of forgiving and building a new life without the man she loved and with whom she had spent more than twenty years. She questioned all those years: *Did he ever love me? Why wasn't I enough for him? Why did he have to look elsewhere? Were all those years a lie?*

It was a process, allowing the healing to take place. She had to choose to forgive as each memory came up. And in the end, she had to let God be God, resisting the urge to judge. She acknowledged that God was Judge, Jury, and Prosecutor.

"Beloved, do not avenge yourselves, but rather give place to wrath, for it is written, 'Vengeance is Mine, I will repay,' says the Lord." (Romans 12:19)

Affairs of the Mind

Pornography has interrupted many a marriage. Very often, the habit starts in teen years when a boy is trying to sort out his own masculinity. But it is easy to revert back to it when things aren't going well in a man's life. The wife feels devastated and betrayed, believing that something is wrong with her and that she isn't enough for her husband.

General Fantasy

Along with pornography is usually a fantasy life. It is the fantasy life that is so damaging. The images are seared on the brain, playing in living color on the scene of the brain. But unlike a TV set, they can't be turned off so easily. A person becomes bonded to the image that they are focusing on when they reach an orgasm.

Sometimes a married person finds it a lot easier to engage in fantasy rather than try to work on a difficult marriage. Self-gratification becomes more important than expressing love to your spouse. I'm not saying it's easy; I am well aware of the many problems that can drive couples apart. All I'm saying is be willing to work on the relationship in a way that allows the Spirit of God to love your spouse through you.

Consider the fruit of the Spirit as listed in Galatians 5:22–23: *"But the fruit of the Spirit is love, joy, peace, longsuffering, kindness, goodness, faithfulness, gentleness, self-control."* It is the Spirit that produces the fruit.

Our responsibility is to abide in Him, be yielded, submission to Christ in us, where our spirit is so merged into the Spirit of God that we are swallowed up in Him and He loves through us.

- ♦ The first three fruit—love, joy and peace—are our attitudes directed toward God.
- ♦ The next three—longsuffering, kindness and goodness—are attitudes we are to have toward others.
- ♦ The last three—faithfulness, gentleness and self-control—are attributes to be developed in the individual. We must be faithful; no one else can do it for us. We must be gentle; no one else can do it for us. We must be self-controlled; no one else can do it for us.

Having a greater understanding of how we get trapped into these sinful patterns like affairs, pornography, fantasy life, etc. will help us get free.

"For all that is in the world, the lust of the flesh, the lust of the eyes, and the pride of life, is not of the Father but is of the world." (1 John 2:16) There is nothing new under the sun. Look with us to the garden where it all began: *"So when the woman saw that the tree was good for food, that it was pleasant to the eyes, and a tree desirable to make one wise, she took of its fruit and ate. She also gave to her husband with her, and he ate."* (Genesis 3:6) The woman saw that the tree was good for food; she yielded to "the lust of the flesh." She saw that the tree was pleasant to the eyes; she yielded to "the lust of the eyes." She saw that the tree would make one wise; she yielded to "the pride of life."

When we go "window shopping," whether it's a person, a new pair of shoes, or a new house, we come home dissatisfied with what we have. We need to make a covenant with our eyes as a protection from the temptation to sin. *"But each one is tempted when he is drawn away by his own desires and enticed. Then, when desire has conceived, it gives birth to sin, and sin, when it is full-grown, brings forth death. Do not be deceived, my beloved brethren."* (James 1:14–16)

We believe there is a spirit of entitlement that has invaded our land and culture. It ushers in a mentality that says, "I deserve this." Or,

"Everyone else is doing it, why not me too?" "I want what I want and I want it now, why wait?" "I'm entitled, so I have to look out for what is mine."

> *A generation ago, our society was flooded with the slogan, "If it feels good, do it." That kind of thinking has elevated feelings and sensuality over wisdom, morality, and spirituality.*

In contrast, when we watch a movie that was made back in the 50s or earlier, we say, "It was a more innocent time." Remember that it's not immature or naive to be innocent; it's a sign of wisdom and purity. We need to ask God for that wisdom in order to make healthy choices and overcome the tyranny of immediate gratification.

Victory In Jesus

One young man told us of his struggle with images long after he broke the habit of pornography. He said the only way he achieved victory over the habit of masturbation was by wearing a crucifix around his neck. And when an uninvited and unwanted image would pop into his mind, he would redirect his focus to the crucifix and by looking at the slain body of Christ, he replaced one image with another. He then thanked Jesus for dying on the cross so that he could be forgiven and be set free from his sin.

May the Lord Jesus Christ make us holy, as He is holy. May we be restored to innocence and purity as is pleasing to Him. Our Lord is returning for a bride without spot or wrinkle, cleansed by the blood of Jesus.

❧ Prayer for cleansing and healing of sexual sin

Father God, in the name of Your Son, Jesus I come before You and humbly ask to be cleansed, set free, and healed of every sexual sin in my life. Forgive me of every wrongful sexual act, in word or deed, thought or fantasy. I have perverted the precious gift of my sexuality and used it in ways that are sinful.

Bring to death in me the habits that keep me sinning. Renew my mind with truth according to Your Word. Cleanse me from every unholy and unlawful touch, to me and to others by me. Cleanse my mind of the fanciful images that are not of You.

I confess my dependence on You, for on my own I cannot keep myself from sinning against You, myself and others. Take the mighty sword of Your Spirit and severe my spirit from every thing and every person that I have unlawfully bonded myself to. I choose to forgive those that have sinned against me from my childhood until now. Heal those hurtful memories within me; my mind, my body, my feelings, and my sexuality.

I ask that You would make Romans 12:1–2 a reality in my life: "I beseech you therefore, brethren, by the mercies of God, that you present your bodies a living sacrifice, holy, acceptable to God, which is your reasonable service. And do not be conformed to this world, but be transformed by the renewing of your mind, that you may prove what is that good and acceptable and perfect will of God."

Accept this prayer, O God and have mercy on me. Amen

6

How a Habit Becomes an Addiction

We know a man who has maintained his sobriety for more than a decade and has sponsored many other men to help them get sober. He told us that it was through attending Alcoholic Anonymous meetings that he came to know the Lord. He said it helped him to see that he had an unhealthy relationship with alcohol. It was familiar; he remembered how when he was growing up, his father would have buddies over to play cards and they would drink. All family celebrations had alcohol served. So it seemed natural for him to drink, but it began to ruin his life. He told us that he learned in AA that first, "a man takes a drink." Then "the drink takes a drink." And the final stage was, "the drink takes the man." He said when he first took a drink it was his own choice, sometimes just with friends; everyone was doing it. Personally he could take it or leave it. But after a while, he began to crave a drink. It didn't matter if others were around or not. Then when he hit the third stage—"the drink takes the man"—he knew he was in real trouble because he couldn't stop no matter how many times he tried. That's when he finally went to AA.

AA found out that through the years, if they could get a person to attend 90 meetings in 90 days, that person would stay sober. Now we know scientifically that it takes 90 days without alcohol before the damage to the brain cells can begin to heal. Until that happens, the person will crave the alcohol.

There is a process by which a habit becomes an addiction. You could say that it's like building a fortress. Every time we indulge in our habit, we're adding another log to this wall that will eventually become the fortress. In other words, our habit lives in a habitation; it has a life of its own and we have built the fortress for it to live in so it can continue to torment and rule us.

When that which was a habit becomes an addiction, the person must seek help from those who have been there. We recommend a 12-Step support group like Celebrate Recovery, AA or other biblically based support groups. Acknowledging that we are powerless to overcome our addiction is the first step toward getting free. Confession of sin and asking forgiveness of those we have hurt is necessary before trust can be restored and the hard work of healing can begin.

It's About Pain

All addictions are about pain. They begin with pain, whether physical or emotional. Maybe there was a physical pain for which prescription drugs offered some relief. But when we have to have more and more to release the pain, an addiction can form. Or maybe there was inner pain; in that case the addiction serves to distract from the emotional issues; it's something that numbs out the inner pain. But then it develops that life of its own and creates more pain…

It helps to look at addiction as something with which we have developed a relationship. If we have a friend who stabs us in the back and tells lies, we don't want to continue in that relationship. So too, the relationship with the addiction is something we don't want to cultivate.

What do you do to numb your pain or take your mind off your troubles? In my (Shelvy's) family, food was the "drug of choice." Milk and cookies made the skinned knee feel better. Good grades were celebrated with food. As soon as visitors walked in the door, they were offered something to eat or drink.

An emotional pain that seems too much to bear? We seek relief. Many times we reach for what is familiar. It may be food or it may be something more harmful. Some parents give food or offer quick entertainment when they are unable or unwilling to give affection or emotional support.

Shopping can be a distraction from an inner pain. Working all the time and staying busy can be an escape from inner pain. Anything can become an addiction when we develop a dependency upon it. There is nothing wrong with shopping, work, food or prescribed medication...but when we can't live without it, we're in trouble.

If a person decides to give up their addiction, it sounds good. But if they don't get to the root of their pain, they will simply trade one dependency for another. When we put someone in a god-like position in our life, it is called co-dependency. When we put anything or any activity in a god-like position in our life, it is called an addiction. God wants to meet every need we have. We have seen women stay in abusive relationships because they couldn't stand the thought of being alone. Some would call it a "love addiction" but it is not love. It might be a woman who thinks she has to have a man in her life at all times. It may just as easily be a man who must have a woman to make him feel good about himself. Sometimes it's a "needy woman" so he can be the rescuer. There are many forms that addiction can take; we've named just a few.

Sometimes the inner pain is so great, the person adds one addiction to another. Like the man who had an addiction to alcohol, then added illegal drugs, then strip clubs and prostitution. He ended up in big trouble and with a prison term. He lost his wife and children. It was such a high price to pay.

Our Lord hurts for us and wants to heal our pain and set us free from every dependency. He wants us to depend on Him.

Addiction Retreat

It was a beautiful stone lodge, filled to capacity; 114 people assembled to attend the retreat. We were anticipating a mighty move of God, and had a ministry team ready to pray for people. There was a waiting list of people who wanted to be there, but we didn't have any more rooms in the lodge. What was God up to?

It was the fall of the year.

Leaves were turning beautiful hues of gold, yellow, bronze and red. What a marvel that God could bring such beauty out of something dying. And yet wasn't

that what He was calling us to do? — "Die daily"? —
Die to our sinful habits and addictions?

During a time of prayer over the group, the Lord flashed a picture into my mind, so I (Shelvy) spoke what I saw. I pictured a young man sitting in the middle of the highway. There were cars zooming by on each side of him. I explained that God has a purpose when he gives a Word of Knowledge. It doesn't matter if it's in words or pictures. He always wants to heal and set us free from our bondages. Sometimes it's painful memories that need to be healed. Sometimes we develop sinful and harmful habits to try to escape the pains of the past. After the meeting concluded, a young man and his wife came up to us. The young man said, "That was me sitting in the middle of the highway." This is the story he told us:

He was a teenager and out drinking with his buddy. "In fact, I'd had too much to drink and wrecked my convertible. My buddy went flying through the air and landed in the middle of the road. As soon as I could get out of the car, I ran to him. I held him in my arms as he died while I sat in the middle of the road."

He hung his head as tears ran down his shame-filled face. Jim put his arm around him to comfort him and let the tears flow.

A few days after the retreat, the couple called for an appointment to come see us. When they arrived, I was amazed that the Lord had filled our hearts with His love and compassion for the young man. We honestly wondered what that was all about.

The young housewife was busy with their children and a part time job, which she worked while the children were in school. She complained that her husband had a "girlfriend" whose name was alcohol and drugs. He spent more time with the "girlfriend" than with her. This young wife missed her husband and wanted him back.

This is the rest of their story that unfolded over the months that we saw them: His father had left when he was three or four years old. The father lived across the country, so the boy rarely saw his him. His mother had a boyfriend and was gone a lot of the time, leaving him and his younger sister with a teenage girl babysitter. One night, the babysitter's boyfriend showed up and they began to argue and then fight. The girl fell and hit her head on the fireplace hearth. He remembered how frightened he was as the blood flowed from her head. His little sister was crying and he tried to hold her and comfort her but he was just a preschooler himself. The babysitter died and in his child's mind he kept thinking maybe there was something he should have done to help her.

Needless to say, there were many painful memories in him. One by one, we tried to speak truth to him and invited the Lord to heal. But progress was slow and he continued to act out. He told us he couldn't seem to stop himself. He worked hard and that kept his mind busy during the day, but when he got off work he felt he deserved to a have a few "cool ones" (alcohol) before heading home. Most Friday evenings until Sunday evening, his wife and children didn't see him.

The progression of his addictions went like this: a few beers, then a few "shots" (stronger alcohol) and then he started adding cocaine. To obtain the drugs he had to go into a very rough part of town, so he carried a gun to protect himself.

The last time we saw him, we said to him: "If you don't stop this addiction and let the Lord complete the work He has begun in you, you are going to wind up dead or in prison." This was not a threat; it was a simple matter of our seeing the path he was on. As you can recall, the Lord had revealed to me that picture of him from a traumatic time in his past; that revelation in itself was striking evidence of God's active communication and desire to set this man free.

However the next thing we heard, he had been arrested for attempted murder during a drug deal that went bad. He was sentenced to a lengthy prison term.

Many of the people we have counseled have been willing and able to receive the healing they needed; their stories have happy endings. Our hearts rejoice when we see them overcome. Just the same, our hearts ache when we hear bad news about those who did not overcome but succumbed once again to old habits and destructive patterns. Sometimes the pain seems overwhelming to them, and then when addiction is added to the equation, there is a tipping point.

> *The simple choices we make in life—to receive God's help or not—can change our destinies for better or worse.*

Regrets: If Only…

"If only…

"If only I had said…

"If only I had done…

"If only I had *not* said…

"If only I had *not* done…

When "If only" comes, the regrets come.

The 35-year-old woman was still blaming herself when she said to me, "I was in junior high school, and every time my mother had too much to drink, she was an embarrassment to me. I didn't want my friends to see and know. I wanted it to remain my secret. Whenever I didn't do what she wanted me to do when she wanted me to do it, she would yell to me, "I'm going to kill myself and then you'll be sorry." One morning when I was in a rush to leave for school, the same scene was replayed.

But this time, I yelled back, "Well, go on and do it and get it over with!" When I returned home from school that afternoon, I found my mother dead from an overdose of pills and alcohol. If only…"

Now years later, the alcoholic husband of this same woman had left her and their children. She was blaming herself for the fact that the children would grow up without a father. What could she have done differently? Maybe it was actually her fault that he drank. That's what he said. Maybe she was a "nag" like he said and that's why he didn't like to come home. On and on she went with her regrets until I said, "You don't have that much power."

"What do you mean?" she said.

I explained that when she was in junior high school, she lacked the power to cause her mother to take her own life, no matter what she said or didn't say. Only her mother had that power over her own life. "And you don't have the power to make your husband drink," I told her. Al-Anon, a support group for people in relationship with alcoholics, has a saying: "You didn't cause it; you can't cure it; you can't control it. Now, let's talk about you."

For more than 20 years, this dear woman had believed she had caused her mother's death. She blamed herself and believed the lie that she had possessed the power to keep her mother alive or to kill her. The process of healing began as she entrusted me with her dark secret. Helping her see with her adult mind that she was not responsible for her mother's actions was a major victory.

We talked also about how it takes two to make a marriage successful and it requires both partners to take responsibility for their own actions and attitudes. Now she was ready to hear God's truths that would set her free.

It wasn't by accident or chance that the patterns of being in relationship with an alcoholic and abandonment were repeated in her life. Her mother, a primary relationship, had written a message on her heart about life—her life. And now, her husband was repeating the pattern. While her mother and her husband were responsible for their own decisions and actions, I needed to help her understand why this was happening to her.

For as he thinks in his heart, so is he. (Proverbs 23:7)

Keep your heart with all diligence, for out of it spring the issues of life. (Proverbs 4:23)

Parents have power and authority, so when her mother said she was no good, then she figured it must be so. As with this woman, she believed that in her mother's own way, she loved her. So, when the alcoholic husband came into her life, love was packaged the same way; it was familiar. She believed him when he said he loved her.

The law of sowing and reaping was at work in her life. The root cause of the pain and difficulty in her life came from the seeds sown in her heart as a child and teen. The fruit was produced in season, when she was a woman, wife and mother. Only the Lord can lay the axe to these roots so they do not continue to produce this kind of fruit.

Therefore bear fruits worthy of repentance... And even now the ax is laid to the root of the trees. (Matthew 3:8,10)

In the weeks that followed, the Lord renewed her heart and mind with truth about what she was responsible for and what she was not. She gave God permission to search her heart and reveal all that was displeasing to Him. The Lord is now cleansing her heart and mind of blame and shame, self-hatred and condemnation, and He is writing a new message on her heart that lines up with His Word, full of His healing and forgiveness and the transforming power of His love!

When You're In a Relationship With an Addict

She was a gentle soul, dressed neatly, good manners and eager to talk. Her co-worker invited her to church a few months ago and she had come to know the Lord in a personal way. She loved the Bible studies, worship services, and women's group. She was hungry to know more and grow as a new believer. She had not received much comfort from her childhood religion, although she had tried to be faithful.

Her story began to flow from her. She had been married for five years. It had taken a while before she realized that her husband had a problem. She tried to do everything she could to help him but nothing worked. She worked three jobs during most of their marriage to support them. He was trying to become a professional baseball player. She believed in him and tried to encourage and support him. But when he didn't win or do well and was discouraged, he began to drink more and more.

After one too many times of drinking until he blacked out, she asked him to seek help. He signed himself into a rehab center, stayed for a couple of weeks, then said he didn't need it anymore. That didn't last long; as soon as he went to visit his parents he would start drinking again. Alcohol was a way of life for them and had been for their family for generations. She would call ahead of time and ask them to please not serve alcohol, but it didn't make any difference. His next crash was worst than the last. It was taking more and more alcohol to satisfy him.

Again she asked him to go to rehab and stay the 28 days that would complete their program. He finally gave in to her. She attended the family meeting and Al-Anon. She was receiving a real education, and saw the many ways she was enabling him and not really helping at all. This time he stayed the course and she said they had a couple of wonderful weeks together; it was almost like when they first met.

Then the inevitable happened; it was the anniversary celebration for his parents and you guessed it...he fell off the wagon in a big way. She couldn't watch as the evening progressed, so she left early and went home. She didn't know what time it was when someone brought him home in the middle of the night. He slept until after lunchtime the next day and woke up in a terrible mood. He probably had an awful hangover. He said the only thing for it was a good, strong drink. It didn't stop there. By the time she returned from grocery shopping he was drunk. But this time he became violent, put his fist through the wall, cursing and threatening her and calling her awful names. When he started throwing things at her, she grabbed her keys and purse and left. She knew it was over.

She called her Al0-Anon sponsor and met her at the diner for coffee. The sponsor said, "Maybe it's time to see a lawyer." She knew it was true, but as crazy as it sounds, she still loved him. She filed for divorce and he moved back home with his parents. After a couple of years she felt it was time to get on with her life; coming to know the Lord and developing new relationships at the church has now given her peace and hope.

It Wasn't Gambling; He Had a "System"

A couple came to see us after they had only been married a few months. She had a successful career in the city and he had worked a number of jobs, including several multi-level marketing positions. He appeared to be quite intelligent and we could see she was impressed with that. They wanted our opinion about an agreement they were trying to work through.

He wanted to give up all efforts to earn a living by working because he could make more money gambling. (He didn't like it when we called his activity by that word.) She had supported herself for years and had no problem earning a living. In fact she was confident she could support them. They were trying to agree on how much money he would be given to work his system and earn a fortune for them to enjoy. She had already agreed to a time limit of five years for this venture. It was evident to us that he had sold her a bill of goods. They waited for our opinion, and needless to say he was not happy with our recommendations. He got very angry, and she was hurt that we thought her decisions were not wise.

They left before we could pray with them, but we did pray after they left. We knew the Lord loved them both and wanted their marriage to work. However, after two years, they were divorced.

Addiction of any kind is so consuming, it is like being married to our habit instead of to our spouse.

With that devouring effect, no wonder addiction has ravaged so many marriages. But when we can somehow get a glimpse of our betrothal to God and receive from Him, His love consumes us in a holy way; we aren't enslaved but set free. We aren't defiled but cleansed. We aren't pulled away from those we love and neither are we enmeshed with them. Instead, we're freed up to love them more truly as well as let them go.

ಔ Prayer

God grant me the serenity to accept the things I cannot change, courage to change the things I can and wisdom to know the difference. Living one day at a time enjoying one moment at a time; accepting hardship as a pathway to peace; taking as Jesus did this sinful world as it is not as I would have it; trusting that You will make all things right if I surrender to Your will; so that I may be reasonably happy in this life and supremely happy with You forever in the next. Amen.[1]

---

[1] The Serenity Prayer (written by Reinhold Niebuhr, circa 1933)

7

God of the Second Chance

"God of the Second Chance"—Do you know Him by that name? Have you ever made the biggest mistake of your life and God redeemed it, worked it together for your good?

> *There is nothing too difficult for God. Give Him a chance and see what He will do. You will find that "God of the Second Chance" also becomes "God of the Next Opportunity."*

Let us share a few testimonies of people we have worked with. You know you can't have a test-imony until you are tested...

A Life Redeemed

He had been an alcoholic for more years than he wanted to remember. There was the usual fallout: While he went to AA, his wife refused to go to Al-Anon. She had given up on the marriage after years of neglect from her husband. Now she was the one withdrawing, and she stopped doing anything around the house. He had to do his own cooking and laundry. She started going out drinking and running up credit card debt due to gambling. They tried a few counselors, but she insisted that she did not have a problem and then would quit going. She did not want to change anything about her behavior and was not interested in reconciliation. They became more and more separate. She refused to work and just wanted out. After more than two decades, there was nothing left but a shell of a marriage. She wouldn't do anything, so it was he who finally filed for the divorce.

He had maintained sobriety for a number of years through attending AA meetings. The man he asked to be his sponsor was a Christian. This man not only helped him work through the 12-Step program but also invited him to attend his church. It was in a men's Bible study that he came to know of Jesus, the Son of God. He traded his childhood religion for a personal love relationship with Jesus Christ. He experienced forgiveness for his sins and told us he felt a load of guilt lift off of him. The transformation didn't take place overnight. But he was faithful: attending church, men's Bible study, AA meetings and trying to make amends with his former wife and grown children.

We warned him that women would be pursuing him. Whenever an eligible, godly man appears in the church, there are always women looking for a good man. We suggested that he wait for a year before dating. He understood that was right for him as he felt he needed to be established as a new man.

Soon he told us of attending a social event at church and meeting a woman of "substance." That's what he called her. She had been divorced for many years and had raised her son alone. Now that her son was grown, she had a decent career in which she held a very responsible position. He didn't make any moves to get to know her, other than running into her in group settings.

After a year, he asked her out to dinner and they hit it off. It wasn't long before we could see that love was in bloom. He brought her to see us and talk about their getting married. They both sold their homes and they bought a new nest. What a blessing to attend their wedding. They have opened their home for a Bible study group from their church, and are influencing the lives of many for the kingdom of God. They just celebrated another wedding anniversary. What a Redeemer God is!

Divorced Couple Remarries... Each Other!

We have been privileged to work with three divorced couples and witness them remarry each other. We want to tell you about one of those couples.

I (Shelvy) heard it before I saw it: An 18-wheeler tractor-trailer pulling up in front of our house. I watched as the driver made his way up to our front door. I thought he was lost and would be asking directions. It seemed strange, though, because we were the last house on a private dead-end road of only four houses. As I answered the doorbell, I was ready to call for Jim because he is better at giving directions than I am. Much to my surprise, the man identified himself as Joe (not his real name) and said he had called for a counseling appointment for that afternoon.

As we sat in our living room and talked, his story unfolded. Joe described himself in his youthful years as a "hell-raiser." Working as a truck driver, he finally landed a stable job for a moving company. He kept looking for excuses to talk to the young woman who worked in the office. Before long, they became friends. She was unlike the other girls he partied with. He could "talk" to her. Their friendship grew into love and they married. Over several years, they'd had three children. But somewhere along the way, they had stopped talking, stopped connecting. The distance between them had grown greater and colder.

In frustration, his temper would flare and he'd say hurtful things that he later regretted. But it was always too late. Anger and frustration would override any attempts to make things better. Finally, he left and filed for a divorce. Freedom did not give him the new lease on life he thought it would.

Later he ran into an old drinking buddy who had been out of his life for more than a decade. "I know everyone changes over time," he said, "but this guy had *really* changed. It wasn't just that he didn't drink anymore. He was different, and I found myself telling him everything that was going wrong in my life."

As Joe continued telling us of this "chance encounter," we knew it was anything but, for we saw that it had the fingerprints of God all over it. What wisdom this long-ago buddy had – he waited until Joe asked what had happened to him, and then it was his turn to tell his story. He had hit bottom, and when he looked up, God had been there waiting for him all the time. He explained how he "dumped the truck" of his old life and asked Jesus to come in and rescue him from a life of destruction. His AA sponsor invited him to his church, where he met loving and caring people.

The following Sunday, Joe went to church with his buddy and he, too, began a life of transformation. As he grew in the Lord, he longed for his former wife to know the same peace that he had found. He went to her and tried to tell her what had happened to him and to say he was sorry. But she was hurt and didn't trust him. His temper flared again and he felt he had really "blown it."

When Joe came to see us, it had been about two years since the divorce. He had repented before the Lord for hurting his wife and children and desired to make amends. He said, "I miss my best friend! I know that I love her more now than when we were married, but how can I get her to trust me again?" We felt it best to just let him talk, get it all out before we gave him our counsel. With tears swimming in his eyes, he said, "I just want a chance to spend time with her so she can see that I have changed. And I want her to know the Lord the way I do. What should I do?"

We invited the Lord's holy presence as we began to pray with Joe. We saw the Lord's love washing over Joe, healing and comforting him. We felt the Father's compassion for a young boy who had never been fathered. Jim spoke words of affirmation from the Father heart of God to Joe.

> *Tears of repentance flowed as Joe realized how he had not been there for his own children. He asked God to give him another chance to be the godly husband and father he knew God wanted him to be. Like a little child, he prayed, "God show me what to do and I'll do it."*

We closed the prayer time by pronouncing absolution for forgiveness of sin: "You are forgiven by the shed blood of Jesus; your sins are absolved."

Later that night, Joe called us. "When I got home, there was a message on my answering machine from my wife," he said, not referring to her as his former wife. "She was inviting me to come Sunday afternoon to see the children. I think it's an answer to our prayers." We agreed and prayed with him that the Lord would go before him and prepare her heart to receive him.

A few weeks later, Joe and his former wife Debbie sat in our living room to begin the first of a series of counseling prayer sessions. Slowly, healing and reconciliation began to take place as trust was restored. Not only did she give her life to the Lord, but all of their children did as well. In the sessions that followed, we identified the root issues in each of their lives. They took responsibility for the baggage each had brought into the marriage. Then, we went to the difficult work of corporate issues. Joe did the hard work on anger management. And Debbie learned, with God's help, to remain open to communication and not let Joe's anger shut her down. They felt the satisfaction of rebuilding their lives and especially, their friendship, which had been the foundation of their relationship.

The day came when they were ready to make a renewed commitment of marriage. What a blessing for us to attend their wedding and see the children stand up as witnesses for their parents to remarry. I don't think there was a dry eye in the church; they shared the events of the last three years before the ceremony, and gave God all the credit for the reconciliation and for the new life He had given them. To God be the glory!

Restoration: God's Re-parenting of a Couple

She was pregnant; he was angry. They weren't married.

He loved her but things never worked out for him. His drug-addicted mother had given him away. Who knew who his father was. He'd lived in one foster home after another until the last one adopted him. He was a young teen with a chip on his shoulder so big he could hardly walk straight. He'd gone to church with his adoptive family, but if God was so good, how come his life was such torment? Alcohol didn't help much to escape the constant pain. He was "no good"—everyone said so. He'd barely made it out of high school and worked construction. Life was pretty meaningless.

Then, he met her—in a neighborhood bar. She was pretty and she talked to him. Of course he was thinking, *if you really knew me, you wouldn't like me.* But for some strange reason, when he asked for her phone number, she gave it to him.

From her perspective, what else was there to do on a Saturday night but hang out at the local bar and hope to meet some decent guy—if there were any out there? It was just her and her mother at home. Dad had flown the coop a long time ago. Mother's boyfriends had changed every now and then, but not much else. She had finished high school and was taking classes at the local community college. She didn't know what she wanted to do with her life, except, some day, get married and have a couple of kids. Maybe that's why she worked at the Day Care. She loved kids.

She had grown up knowing that "you can't count on the man"—the "woman has to be strong." So what was it about him that attracted her so much? Sure, he was cute, but there was something else. She saw a deep loneliness that made her want to hug and comfort him.

She knew he was holding back that night in the bar, but that was okay; she could talk enough for both of them. When he asked for her phone number, she wanted to shout, "YES, YES!" But of course she didn't.

The next day, he called and she met him. It wasn't long before they were seeing each other every day. They were so much in love; they couldn't stay away from each other.

When she found out she was going to have his baby, she was thrilled. Now she'd have a *real* family: a husband, children, and a home of her own.

However it didn't turn out that way. Not only was he not thrilled, he was angry. "How could you be so stupid as to let yourself get pregnant?" he ranted.

"Like I did it all by myself!" she said.

She didn't hear from him for a few days. She told her mother and they cried together. Her mother assured her, she and the baby would always have a home with her. And she added a reminder, "You know how men are, you can't count on them."

After a few weeks, he came around, apologizing that he didn't mean those things he'd said. He loved her and wanted to marry her. They had a quiet ceremony by a Justice of the Peace. He moved from his adoptive parents' home to her mother's home.

They both worked hard to buy the things necessary for a new baby. She dropped out of her college classes. He didn't always come straight home from work but stopped at the bar "to have a few cold ones." They would have *words* on occasion but nothing really changed; they both seemed to stay angry.

The hardest part for her was that she was lonely; she couldn't get him to really talk to her. She just wanted him, wanted to be with him. After their son was born, she had less and less time for her husband.

He wasn't ready for all this responsibility; it frightened him to think he had a wife and child depending on him. All they seemed to do was fight over money. She wanted their own place to live; that meant move out of her mother's home where they were only paying for utilities and food. How could they ever pay a rent or a mortgage?

They had no sooner celebrated their son's first birthday when she told him she was pregnant again. Even though she too was worried about the money, she was happy to be having another child. He didn't even fight this time—just left and got drunk. She didn't see him for several days. He came home more withdrawn than ever.

When their second son was born, she had her hands full. He didn't seem to know what to do to help but he worked hard on his construction job. Coming home to two noisy toddlers and two yakking women night after night, finally he couldn't take it anymore. He left.

His sister and her husband let him stay with them, temporarily. They told him about Jim, and he came for counseling.

Jim ministered the Father's love to this young man. Salvation and healing began to flow into him like water in a dry desert. As he worked through the process of forgiveness, he was being set free of his judgments, inner vows and expectations. Soon he wanted his wife back, but she had given up on him and gotten a divorce.

She hadn't wanted a divorce; she loved him and believed in him more than he believed in himself. But she didn't know what else to do; they couldn't talk and nothing had ever changed.

He came to see the boys and also to give her money. He seemed different—more at peace—especially now that he'd given up smoking and drinking. He asked her to go with him to see us for marriage counseling. Did she dare hope that they could be together again?

We saw them a few times, and they began to talk—connecting, spending time rediscovering the love that had always been there. Forgiveness flowed as understanding broke through.

He moved back in with her and the boys. They went to a Justice of the Peace and remarried.

We continue to work with them to help them manage their money better and get a home of their own. We'll be mentoring them as a couple to teach them how to nurture their relationship and also how to parent their sons.

Is anything too difficult for God? They had it all—so many issues! Unwed pregnancy, anger, drug addicted mother, adoption, drinking, abandonment by father, female dependency, loneliness, money issues, unplanned pregnancy, separation, divorce; need for salvation, counseling, healing, forgiveness, remarriage, mentoring… the works! God re-parented these young parents and taught them how to love each other through all their circumstances.

What a joy to see the Lord's healing hand at work in this couple and their family! His love does cover a multitude of sins, and His love never fails.

Perhaps you want to know the "God of the Second Chance" and experience His redeeming love in your life. Rest assured there is no sin, mistake, wounding or abuse that is greater than God's ability to redeem it. Pray with us:

✺ Prayer

Father God, I come before You confessing that I have made a mess of my life. I feel my life is an ash-heap; I have burnt so many bridges behind me. Forgive me Lord, for every way I have sinned against You, others and myself. You know the areas where I need a second chance. I confess You are the God of the impossible and nothing is too difficult for You. Bring to death in me all unbelief and doubt that You would do this for me. I want to come into alignment with Your plans for my life. Enter into the circumstances of my life and manifest Yourself in such a way as to bring glory and honor to You. I desire to fulfill all Your purposes for my life and come into my destiny. Write a new message on my heart that Your love is greater than my sin. I trust in You. In Jesus' name, Amen.

8

Male and Female Abusers

Living With Misogyny

I (Shelvy) hesitate to share this portion of my story, but it shaped so much of my life for more than 25 years that I feel I must. I want to tell what it is like to live with misogyny. One warm and beautiful summer evening, my first husband and I went to a favorite Virginia Beach restaurant for dinner. As was his custom, he parked his luxury Lincoln automobile in a parking space that was the furthest from the entrance. He wanted to make sure no one parked next to us for fear they would open a car door and hit his car. I had accepted this trait in him, so I didn't say anything.

After we finished eating at the restaurant, we were walking back to the car when all of a sudden he started cursing and became enraged. I had no idea what set him off. Then I saw that someone had parked next to our car. Before inspecting his car to see if there were any scratches or dents, he took out his car keys and jammed the key into the driver's door as hard as he could. Then he proceeded to drag the key down the entire side of the car, leaving an ugly, deep scratch. He had just done the very thing he feared someone would do to him. He continued to rage all the way home. Once the car was back in the garage, he took a flashlight and inspected the car inch by inch. He never said so but I knew he never found a single scratch or dent.

I had learned the hard way about his unreasonableness concerning the car. Not long after he purchased it, I discovered where it was on his list of priorities. It was a rainy night in September and I was about to leave for the parent-teacher's meeting at our children's school. I was looking forward to meeting their teachers for the first time. He announced to me that he had to go out and he was driving my station wagon; "You can call a friend and get a ride to the school." That made no sense to me. Sitting in our garage was his expensive new car. When I asked if there was something wrong with his car, he almost bit my head off, saying, "I'm not taking my car out in the rain and get rain spots all over it. You can get a ride with one of your 'precious' friends!" That comment about my friends was said sarcastically because he wouldn't let anyone close enough to him to be a friend and was angry that I had.

The memory of what he did to that car in the restaurant parking lot made me afraid to say another word. I simply picked up the telephone and called a friend and asked for a ride to the school.

It would be years before I even heard the word "misogyny," much less understand what it meant. Misogyny comes from the Greek "miso" meaning to hate, and "gyn," which means woman. The "hatred of woman" is to devalue and dishonor her. The breeding ground for misogyny is what we refer to as "female dependency." It happens when a boy is dependent upon his mother because of the absence, neglect or abusiveness of the father, or because what the father models as manhood is not acceptable for the boy. For whatever reason, the father is not there to parent the boy and, at the appropriate time, help cut the boy free from mother's controls and launch him to make it on his own. As mother becomes his "all in all," the boy develops ambivalent attitudes toward her. He loves her because she is always there for him, and hates her because she controls him—or he thinks she does. He needs her and is afraid he can't make it on his own.

My first husband's father was a Navy officer and was gone at sea much of the time he was growing up. Also, given that his father was domineering and controlling, what his son saw modeled was oppressive. His father ruled the home the way he ruled his ship. His mother had all the responsibility while the father was gone. But the minute his father came home, she had to take the back seat while he demeaned and dishonored her.

All of his sense of security came from his mother because she was the one who was there all the time. His father did not affirm him or teach him how to make it in the world apart from a woman. My husband didn't want to hurt his wife the way he had seen his father hurt his mother. However, because he refused to forgive his father and instead had judged him, causing him to dishonor his father in his heart, it did not go well with him. He became just like his father after all.

Therefore you are inexcusable, O man, whoever you are who judge, for in whatever you judge another you condemn yourself; for you who judge practice the same things. (Romans 2:1)

Honor your father and mother, which is the first commandment with promise: that it may be well with you and you may live long on the earth. (Ephesians 6:2–3)

When we were married, he simply projected onto me, as his wife, all his unresolved mother issues. He loved me as his wife, but he also hated me. He needed me to be perfect so his world would be perfect. I was flattered by his attentiveness while we were dating. I was so naïve as to believe his jealousy was because he loved me so much. I would later come to realize his jealousy came out of his own insecurities.

One of my most painful experiences came when I had pneumonia. I was so weak I was on all fours just to make it to the bathroom. As I returned to my bed, my head was spinning from the exertion. When my husband came home from work he always wanted his dinner on the table and ready to eat. However this time I was too sick to cook. He came into the bedroom and stood over me, cursing and calling me lazy because his dinner wasn't ready. All I could think at the time was, *why does he hate me so much?* I didn't understand that his sense of security was tied up in me. He needed me to keep his world on schedule because then he felt in control.

> *It would be years before I discovered what it was in me that had caused me to marry a man who would treat me like that. On a heart level, I believed I deserved poor treatment.*

Having received rejection in the womb, then being molested at an early age as well as suffering from an undiagnosed learning disability, I was set up for low self-esteem. I didn't like me very much. I didn't feel attractive or smart. I wanted so much to be loved and accepted that I was flattered by all the attention and gifts given to me during our courtship. But that ended fast. After we were married, it seemed everything I did was wrong. That became just like when I was in school. I just kept trying harder and harder, all the while trying to project the image of the girl "Most Likely to Succeed" (what I was voted by my graduating class). Yet my wounds kept me in bondage to him.

After living with a man with misogynistic behavior and attitudes in which the woman is to blame for everything, I was convinced that I was a terrible person. He'd say, "You're lucky I put up with you."

I began to think, *I must be crazy.* I tried so hard to please him. I would do whatever it took to live at peace. I was so confused. When I would do what he told me and then it did not turn out well, he would blame me and deny what he had said.

Out of desperation, I looked in the phone book and found a psychologist and made an appointment. Of course, I could not let my husband know, but I had to find out if I really was losing my mind. Since he controlled the money, I had none of my own. I started saving a few dollars each week from the grocery money and when I had the amount the psychologist charged, I went to see him.

I answered all his questions about my background, my husband's background and current circumstances. He then explained to me that I was not losing my mind. He explained my husband's dependence on his mother in the absence of his father. Also, how that ambivalence was transferred onto me, as it would have been to anyone he married. That information made me feel better. Here was someone who understood what I was living with, year after year.

He said, "He has to keep everything under control, especially you, because his security, his very world, hinges on you holding it all together, just as it had with his mother. He lacks confidence in himself because his father was not there for him but demanded that he perform without giving him the confidence or inner strength to do so."

His explanations were wondrously helpful to me, but then he lowered the boom: "Should you decide to leave him, I caution you to first consider what effect it would have on him. I strongly suspect that he would take his own life because he has had a lifetime of total dependence on women and he's probably convinced he could not make it without one. So if you think you can live with that consequence, you are free to leave." I felt like saying, "Thanks a lot! I am anything but free!"—for I knew I could not live with that.

Having lived with this misogynistic spirit for so many years, I can spot it a mile away. I was food shopping and standing in line at the deli counter when I heard a little old man berating his wife. He was emotionally and verbally abusing her, and she just stood there with her head hanging down. His face was turned toward her and all I saw was the back of his head. I started praying and staring at the back of his head until he turned around and looked at me. I didn't say a word but in my spirit I was saying, *Shame on you!* He never said another word.

According to Scripture, men who don't treat their wives well and don't respect them could be keeping their own prayers from being answered.

Husbands, likewise, dwell with them with understanding, giving honor to your wife, as to the weaker vessel, and as being heirs together of the grace of life, that your prayers may not be hindered. (I Peter 3:7)

Recently, Jim and I were returning home from a long flight. After the plane taxied up to the gate and we were getting ready to depart the plane, we heard a loud voice coming from the back. A man who looked like he had had too much to drink was standing in the aisle, cursing the woman standing with him. He was verbally abusing her by cursing and calling her names. Everyone around them was embarrassed. She didn't answer him, just gathered up her things and started moving down the aisle. As soon as the man stepped off the airplane, he was met by four uniformed officers and placed under arrest. That's what needs to happen to every abuser, male or female.

Female Dependency

"You shall not make for yourself a carved image [an idol]—any likeness of anything that is in heaven above, or that is in the earth beneath, or that is in the waters under the earth; you shall not bow down to them or serve them. For I, the Lord your God, am a jealous God, visiting the iniquity of the fathers upon the children to the third and fourth generation of those who

hate Me, but showing mercy to thousands, to those who love Me and keep My commandments." (Exodus 20: 4–6)

None of us would think that we were into idol worship. But that is exactly what female dependency is. When a boy grows up without a father, as this man did, he looks to his mother to meet all his needs. He looks to the woman to tell him how he's doing and to make him feel good about himself. He always has to have a woman in his life so if his wife is not available to him it's easy for him to look elsewhere. Anything we put in a god-like position in our lives becomes an idol. When we look to another to meet our needs instead of looking to God, we have entered into an idolatrous relationship. Whether it's a person, work, drugs, alcohol, food, or anything else that we are dependant on rather than God, we have entered into a relationship of dependency. God wants us to depend on Him.

In the second chapter of Genesis, God instructed Adam to not eat of the tree of the knowledge of good and evil. Man would enter into self-rule, being independent; he would have no need to ask God about anything.

"And my God shall supply all your needs according to His riches in glory by Christ Jesus." (Philippians 4:19)

Interdependency In Marriage

When two people marry, they move into their new roles as husband and wife. They develop interdependency with each other. They look to each other to meet certain needs that only a spouse can meet. But our spouses can never be our all-in-all. They cannot be our *Everything*, for that is idolatry. Sometimes, children raised by a mom on her own never have the "apron strings" severed. Even into marriage, some adult children look to their mother in ways that are inappropriate.

One couple was married a few years before they had a child. After their child was born, they were both looking forward to the time they could resume their sexual intimacy. But it didn't turn out the way they thought it would. He was raised by a single mom who had looked to him as an emotional substitute mate, giving him the affection and attention that was a little too much. As a teen, he felt very uncomfortable when she would hug and cling to him, calling him pet names. His mother thought nothing of coming out of the shower with only a towel wrapped around herself. As a teen boy, his body would respond and he quickly shut down and looked away.

So when this couple tried to reconnect after the birth of their baby, he had difficulty performing. Finally he jumped out of bed, shouting, "You can't make love to someone's mother!"

His wife was now a mother, and that role shift had set up all kinds of problems for him. After years of telling his body to shut down at the sight of his near naked mother, it was as if an inner vow had been made—"You can't make love to someone's mother." This mindset and behavior were so deeply ingrained in him along with other issues in the marriage that this couple ended up getting a divorce. Sad to say, another marriage destroyed.

"I Am Doing A New Thing"

We counseled a woman (we'll call her Lucy) whose husband was a full-blown misogynist, both verbally and physically abusive. He not only put her down constantly, criticizing everything she did, but he'd put holes in their doors and walls and grabbed his wife by the head, punched her and thrown her across the room. All the while justifying it by quoting scripture and saying she wasn't "submitting" to him properly. Lucy and her husband had three young children whose lives would have been in serious trouble if not for the Lord's intervention.

When she first came to us, Lucy was tightly bound up, afraid of her own shadow. She wore clothes that hid her form and she stood with her head hanging slightly. We could see that she was an intelligent and gifted woman, but she'd gone "underground," allowing her personality to all but disappear in the years she'd been married. Her world had shrunk down so far that she'd become isolated; she'd lost many friends, didn't do anything without her husband's permission, and couldn't even walk around the block without reporting constantly to her husband on a walkie-talkie that he'd purchased "for her protection."

When I suggested to her that she was enabling her husband, she asked what that meant. "It's the same as if he were a drug addict," I explained to her, "except in his case it's the abuse. If he were addicted to heroin, what you're doing is handing him the needle." As I began to lead her in prayer, Lucy broke down and wailed with grief.

It took some time for Lucy to trust us at first; her fear of setting her husband off caused her to hesitate when it came to receiving anyone's help, so her progress came in fits and starts. She'd come for a few counseling sessions and then withdraw, disappearing for several months. As always, the healing she needed did not just involve the circumstances of her marriage but also issues from her original family—all those messages on her heart that had led her into that abusive situation in the first place. Fortunately Lucy's desperation eventually drove her to trust the Lord enough to work with us and she committed to receiving more help with the deeper healing she so sorely needed.

As we counseled Lucy, she began to grow strong enough to draw some healthy boundaries. She took steps to put herself and her children in a safer position, and she gradually learned how to stop caving in to her husband's constant pressure. With the help of many who were praying for Lucy, the day came when she no longer allowed her husband to abuse her—she told him to leave the house. While Lucy and her husband were separated, he was unwilling to seek further healing during that time. We've found that in cases of misogyny, many are unwilling to go through the painful process of receiving the healing they need.

She didn't want a divorce, but after over two years of waiting and praying, Lucy sensed she needed to let go. She knew divorce wasn't something that delighted God's heart; however by this time Lucy also understood that it would not be God's will for her to subject herself and her children to further abuse.

As a single mother, Lucy grew by leaps and bounds; her children began to heal and flourish in the new peace that flooded their home. They all experienced a personal renaissance, venturing to do those things that they hadn't dared to do earlier for fear Lucy's ex would explode. They even went on a mission trip together, going halfway around the world—what a change from hardly being allowed around the block! Lucy shared with us that this verse from Hosea became very real to her:

"Therefore behold, I will allure her, will lead her into the wilderness, and

speak comfort to her. I will give her her vineyards from there, and the Valley of Achor [trouble] as a door of hope; she shall sing there as in the days of her youth; as in the day when she came up from the land of Egypt. "And it shall be, in that day," declares the Lord, "that you will call Me 'My Husband'; you will no longer call Me 'my Master'." (Hosea 2:14–16)

> *Overcoming trouble in that abusive marriage was the very means by which Lucy discovered new hope, new strength and new fruitfulness in her life. She began to feel that the Lord was indeed her husband.*

Far from being a harsh or distant master, God seemed to be personally opening doors for Lucy right and left, encouraging her to use her gifts and talents and providing for her in miraculous ways.

Lucy hadn't considered getting married again, so she was surprised when months later she found herself distracted by one of the gentlemen in leadership at her church. She served on the same committee with this man and noticed that she was drawn to him, but wasn't sure if God was in it. Not only that, but Lucy couldn't imagine that a man would want to marry her at that stage of life, a single mother of three in her forties!

It was at about this time that Lucy shared a verse in Isaiah that kept standing out to her everywhere she went: *"Do not remember the former things; nor consider the things of old. Behold, I will do a new thing! Now it shall spring forth; shall you not know it? I will even make a road in the wilderness and rivers in the desert." (Isaiah 43:18–19)*

We watched and prayed as finally Lucy could sense God might be preparing her for a new relationship. She explained that while she felt excitement in her spirit, at the same time just the thought of opening up again was painful and brought up underlying fears. The Lord needed to woo her gently through the pain and fear before she was ready for a new relationship. She knew He had good plans for her; she just felt nervous anyway. Lucy set aside "date times" with God in which she'd open her heart to Him and begin to imagine once again sharing her heart with a man—a *safe* man.

As a tentative friendship developed between Lucy and this gentleman, everyone around them could see a deeper relationship forming, long before they were an "item." In fact, family and friends had been praying for years that God would provide a suitable wife for this calm, strong, thoughtful bachelor in his forties. When a match is a good one, it will be affirmed in the Body of Christ and by all who know the couple; such was the case with Lucy and the new husband God had picked out for her.

As we've said earlier, marriage is God's number one refinement tool and He had plenty more work to do in Lucy—as much healing as she'd had already during her years as a single mother. That's another story! But God did indeed do a new thing in Lucy's life, a thing that caused all the other single women around her to ask, "Does he have a brother?"

The Female Shrike

Women, as well as men, do their share of making their marriages miserable. Women tend to be more verbal than men. It begins in early childhood on the playground, where little girls converse in sentences. Boys, on the other hand, tend to make sounds: the roar of an engine, the explosion of a gun being fired, shouts and yells, slams and bangs. What starts out as a gift in the female, being able to articulate her ideas and feelings, turns into a weapon when it's used against the man. Many women conduct themselves like a shrike.

A shrike is a bird described as being sturdily built with a noticeable hook at the tip of its beak. It produces no music but shrill cries. It is recognized by its markings: a black bandit's mask over the eyes. This bird can be spotted on overhead wires or exposed branches. Their prey consists of insects or rodents but mostly other birds, sparrow-sized or smaller. They may be seen hovering over their prey or they may pounce rapidly, with a bite to the back of the head. Their method of storing food is to impale their victims on thorn trees, or barbed wire, and continue to peck them to death. This has given them a ghoulish reputation.

There are women who peck their victims to death with their tongue. A husband will feel he can't win with this kind of woman. She will be negative and critical of everything he does; there is no pleasing her. She does not build up her husband but tears him down. She gathers all the family righteousness to herself. She is the one who is right and seeks to be the authority on what is right, thus she becomes self-righteous.

But no man can tame the tongue. It is an unruly evil, full of deadly poison. With it we bless our God and Father, and with it we curse men, who have been made in the similitude of God. Out of the same mouth proceed blessing and cursing. My brethren, these things ought not to be so. (James 3:8–10)

A soft answer turns away wrath, but a harsh word stirs up anger. The tongue of the wise uses knowledge rightly, but the mouth of fools pours forth foolishness. (Proverbs 15:1–2)

Can You Help My Parents?

This was the question asked of us as we listened to a concerned young woman. She told us that her mother was making her father's life miserable. "She's more than critical, she seems to rip him to shreds every chance she gets and I think he has finally had enough. He's talking about going abroad to see his family and I'm afraid he won't come back."

By the daughter's description of her mother, we felt she was probably acting like a shrike. Sure enough, they were on our couch maybe ten minutes and she had already told us everything he had ever done wrong in the last 45 years. When he tried to talk, she would butt in and talk over him.

We had to explain our ground rules. Only one could talk at a time and we would make sure each got an opportunity to respond. He looked quite relieved.

His story: He wanted to visit his homeland and his family while he was in good health and could travel the distance.

Her story: She didn't want him to spend the money. "That's 'my' money for when you die!"

She was not open to hearing anything we said unless we agreed with her. No, she did not think her negativity could be coming from depression. He was just being selfish.

So the answer to the daughter's question, "Can you help my parents?" was, "No." We did pray, however, that the father would have the inner strength to do what was right for him. Never underestimate the effect that prayers can have! We may be entirely unable to persuade someone of what's right for them, but God knows better than any of us how they might be reached and helped to turn around sooner rather than later.

No Free Lunches

A young man had been coming to see Jim for some time. We were so happy to hear he had met someone. We knew he was lonely; such an intelligent guy but it didn't seem that many understood him. He didn't have a lot of friends.

As the story unfolded, we began to have our doubts about her. She professed to be a Christian. She too was intelligent. They had ended up in his apartment having sex; she stayed the night and never left. He appeared to be overwhelmed that things moved so fast. Next thing we knew, she wanted a ring.

When he brought her to meet us, we feared that she might be a shrike. She was living in his apartment, not working but critical of everything he did. She wasn't just critical of him but of churches also. No one seemed to get it right but her. She felt the need to put him down and lift herself up, bragging about her accomplishments. He felt convicted that it wasn't right for them to have sex and not be married. So they stopped sleeping together.

It appeared to us that she felt she was superior to him and she was doing him a favor by being in his life. When they left our house, we prayed that the Lord would open his eyes to what kind of woman she was. And we asked the Lord to divinely intervene because we knew it would be a huge mistake for him to marry her.

She received a phone call from her former husband and found out that she was still legally married to him. As it turned out, that wasn't the only husband. There were other husbands and other divorces. Thank You, God for rescuing a good man from a shrike!

Job's Wife

Some scholars believe the Old Testament book of Job was the first written book of the Bible. There are many lessons to be learned by studying it. We find a righteous man, having been richly blessed with a large family and large flocks of livestock. Everything is going well until the Lord has a conversation with Satan.

"Then the Lord said to Satan, *"Have you considered My servant Job, that there is none like him on the earth, a blameless and upright man, one who fears God and shuns evil?" (Job 1:8)*

Job is tested to the "max" while one tragedy after another strikes his life. Every thing that he has worked for is wiped out, along with all his children. As his life is crumbling all around him, what is his wife doing? Is she reaching out to comfort him as they deal with all their losses? Is she encouraging him and telling him that she believes in him? Does she remind him that he is a godly and faithful man? Does she tell him that just as God blessed in the past, He will see Job and her through all the calamities that have come upon them? NO! NO! NO! She says to her husband, *"Curse God and die!" (Job 2:9)*

What a negative role model she is! I've never heard a woman say, "I want to be a wife just like Job's wife." And yet, many times we say things to our husbands that are an equivalent of "curse God and die." For the man, it's like being kicked while he's down.

Male or female, abusers are hurt people who hurt people. It can take many forms, but no matter what the circumstances, it's vital for the one being abused to receive enough healing to take a stand. Once we know that we know we are HIS betrothed, we're less likely to put up with anything abusive.

∞ Prayer

Lord, I confess that I have been abused but I have also abused others. Forgive me and bring to death in me those ungodly traits that are not like Christ. I choose to forgive those that have hurt me; I place them in Your hands. I acknowledge that it is hurt people who hurt others. Heal me, Lord. In Jesus' name, Amen.

9

Divorce: When the Dream Dies

Grieving the Loss of the Dream

Whether it's death or divorce, every marriage relationship that ends has to be grieved. We must grieve all losses.

When we were married, Shelvy had been a widow for two years and Jim was divorced for ten years. So we both understand the pain and loss of severing a covenant of marriage.

Sometimes the most difficult loss to grieve is the loss of the "dream." When each couple marries, they have a dream of what they think their life together will be. It's hard to let go of that dream.

Without allowing the Lord to come into our inner man and heal the hurts and disappointments, we become bitter and resentful. We don't have to carry that baggage into another relationship. We don't have to live with the mistakes of the past, whether theirs or ours.

That is why Jesus Christ, the sinless Son of God, willingly became the sacrifice for our sin. When He was crucified on the cross at Calvary, His shed blood enabled us to forgive and be forgiven. What a miracle that the shame and guilt of the past can be cleansed, healed, and forgiven.

The Church And Divorce

Isn't it time the Church lifted the stigma off individuals who are divorced? Divorce is not the unforgivable sin. No, it is not God's best and we would never say that it is, but where is the compassion for the hurting?

Is there any greater pain than to be betrayed, abandoned, or despised? That is what so many people experience through divorce. How could something that began so full of hope and happiness end? No one plans the wedding, walks down the aisle and says, "I do" with any idea that it won't last forever. Pledging a lifetime commitment to love and faithfulness, and then having it severed, cut in two, cut short, all dreams aborted—who can endure such pain, mostly without support or comfort? When a spouse dies, we rush to help and offer comfort and understanding. But when a marriage dies, people choose up sides and decide who to blame for the failure. This should not be! We in the church need to change our attitudes toward all wounded and let God deal with who is to blame or who failed. We need to show the compassion of Christ.

Someone is always quick to say, "God hates divorce." And that's right, He does, but He also hates abuse and a lot of other things.

Some people find themselves divorced and it is not at all what they wanted. In the course of counseling for so many years, we have been asked many questions about divorce:

- ◆ "What kind of god would insist that a woman stay married to a man who has sexually molested their child?"
- ◆ "What about the wife who has committed adultery not once but numerous times?"
- ◆ "What about the able-bodied man who refuses to work and support his family?"
- ◆ "What about the gambler who has a brilliant 'system' but loses all the family's resources?"
- ◆ "What about the man who brings a prostitute into the marriage bed while his wife is out of town?"
- ◆ "What about the man who is not only unfaithful but also fathers a child and continues the adulterous affair?"

We could continue the list, but you get the idea. We as Christians need to show compassion for all wounded.

Marriage Destroyed Or Restored

Our stories of God's courtship would not be complete without a look at the many ways we've seen Him restore marriages. Having read about marriages that are destroyed, you may wonder why something meant to be so full of love and closeness is a source of such pain and strife for so many. The very institution of marriage is under fire in our culture as we write.

One reason for this battle over marriage may have to do with how important it is in God's kingdom. He has called us (the Church) to be His bride; marriage between man and woman on earth is but a picture of the heavenly matrimony we're to have with the Lord. While all that God does is based on relationship, the enemy's mode of operation is always "divide and conquer." He seeks to destroy relationship and takes every opportunity to put a wedge in wherever he can.

Even so, anyone looking to God for help will soon discover that He uses even those difficulties to woo us—not only closer to Himself but also back to those people who love us. The very adversity we face, as we overcome with God's help, becomes a bonding agent and a reminder of God's faithfulness to us in His marriage covenant.

As we showed in Chapter Seven, it has been our privilege to work with four divorced couples who remarried. We use the word "work" because that is what it took to restore each relationship. When a couple is willing to look at their own contributions to the failure of the marriage, take ownership for their own participation and then make amends, we're on our way to healing. Trust must be restored and true repentance offered to the Lord so that forgiveness can be accomplished.

God's way works! Examine the roots and deal with the bad fruit. *Therefore bear fruits worthy of repentance. (Matthew 3:8)*

He Didn't Want a Divorce

This godly man sat before us, broken and grieving. His wife had filed for a divorce and he did not want a divorce. Yes, there were problems in the marriage, but he was willing to work on his issues while she refused to continue to come for counsel. We understood why she was taking such drastic action, but it was not right and certainly was not of God.

She had issues from her family of origin, having been raised in what she saw as poverty. By all we were told, she didn't get the things she wanted but certainly had the essentials provided for her during her childhood. She demonstrated some behaviors that pointed to a personality disorder, but she refused to own her own behavior and did not think she needed help. "He just needs to change." That is what she said to us.

He struggled to protect their children from her extreme behaviors but more often than not, he gave in to her in order to keep peace. She had a problem with hoarding. She believed she must store up "stuff" because if she ever had a need, God would not provide for her. The basement was lined with bags of her purchases. Clothes the children had already outgrown. Clothes that still had the sales tags on them—she had never taken them off. Some of the rooms in their living area were also lined with unopened shopping bags.

We told him it wasn't enough for him to just tithe, which he had done for years. He needed to be a good steward with the ninety percent that was left over. He also needed to be mindful of what was being taught to their children by the example of their parents. He was a hard worker and had always earned a good living. She had never worked outside the home. He tried to talk with her but got nowhere.

So he decided to draw up a budget and presented it to her. He was more than generous in a weekly allowance for her, but she became enraged, saying, "No one is going to tell me what I can spend!" He had never said "No" to her; he'd always bought her the car she wanted, agreed to the home she picked out. He admitted to us that he was at fault for spoiling her. He prayed in front of us, asking God's forgiveness and repenting for "idolizing the woman." Because he had lost his mother at an early age, he just wanted to keep his wife happy.

God instructs parents to "train up" their children in the way they should go, and what was going on in this home was not good training. It certainly did not prepare the children for real life. We do not get to buy everything we want and then fill the basement with unopened bags of merchandise.

While we understood her spending addiction, she needed to be set free from the compulsion to hoard...storing up stuff out of fear of not having enough. The memories of growing up poor and having to go without were very painful for her. All addictions begin with pain, but we don't have to stay in bondage of this habit. The Lord can heal any painful memories and bring to death any bad habits.

What is so ironic is that the very thing she did not want is what she got through the divorce. She was awarded a very generous settlement, but it was set up to put a limit on her spending. The very thing she didn't want—"someone telling her how much she could spend"—is what she got. There is an end in sight; the alimony and child support will end when the children are eighteen years old.

It has been heartbreaking to watch this man go through this second time of abandonment by the primary woman in his life. The first time was when his mother died, and then the woman he loved, the mother of his children, chose to leave him. But through this time alone he has found a deeper relationship with the Lord. He is learning that God is sufficient for every need he has.

I (Shelvy) remember a time (a couple of years later) when he told us of a trip he was taking. As we prayed for him, I felt the Lord say, "He's going to meet his bride." I would not tell him this; what if it wasn't God but my own wishful thinking for him? But I made a note on the bottom of the session notes for that day. After he left, I shared this with Jim and we prayed for him.

It was indeed God speaking. Almost a month later, he told us of meeting a very special godly woman who had never married. Although they lived quite a distance from one another, he wanted to get to know her. He felt this was something God was doing and he was excited to see what the future would hold. Less than a year from the time they met, we were blessed to attend their wedding. God does all things well!

∞ A Prayer of Repentance for a Poverty Spirit

Heavenly Father, I confess that You have created all things. Lovingly and caringly you made us in your image. You have been faithful in caring for all You have created.

With our mouths we have testified, "You supply our needs." But with our hands we have seized your generous blessings to spend them upon ourselves.

We have held tightly to those blessings, hoarding instead of giving, hiding instead of revealing. We confess that a spirit of poverty has gripped our hearts, fear has ruled up despite your promises of supplying all our needs, and despite what you have performed through the ages. We confess that this spirit of poverty wants our death.

Today, we desire to be set free from this fear of not having enough. We desire to be like you, generous on all occasions, believing that you are able to make all grace abound, so that in all things at all times, having all that we need, we will abound in every good work.

Forgive us today of this grievous sin. In holding back our resources, we have denied others your generosity through us. We are impoverished despite your mercy toward us. We reject the work of Satan through this spirit of poverty, and we come in humility to ask You to lift this spirit off of us. We desire to be givers, generous reflections of your Spirit in us. Break the power of this spirit now, in the name of the Lord Jesus. Thank You for the generosity and love of the Lord Jesus in whose name we pray. Amen

ഇ Prayer

Father God, Forgive me for the times I have not shown Your compassion to those who have been wounded by divorce. Forgive me for the unscriptural beliefs that do not line up with Who You are. Take off of me the stigma that the Church projected, making me feel like a second-class citizen in the Kingdom of God. I choose to forgive those in the Church for the ways they have wounded me and others who are hurting. I thank You Lord that You are a Redeemer and there is no life that You cannot redeem. Heal my wounds that divorce has inflicted on my family and me. In Jesus' name I pray, Amen.

10

Life Interrupted

Illness and death are never what we plan for our lives, nor for our spouses and our children. However, the unexpected and unwanted does happen. Nevertheless, God says His grace is sufficient for us and in all circumstances (see 2 Corinthians 12:9).

Marriage Interrupted By Illness and Death

She was a widow of two weeks when she came to see me at her pastor's urging. She was tired and really needed to talk. Her story came pouring out in between tears. She'd met her husband in college. They were both business majors, Christians, and very much in love. They'd been married seven years, both worked hard and had bought a condo.

Then he started having severe headaches. After all the tests and doctors' appointments, they were given the sad news: the diagnosis was a malignant brain tumor. After eighteen months of treatments with everything that was available to fight the inevitable, he slipped from this earthly life into eternity.

She was worn out! She had used up all of her available leave from work taking care of her husband. Many nights she would be up most of the night attending to him, and then have to go to work as soon as the day nurse arrived. He didn't want to leave her but knew his time was drawing to an end.

A few days before he died, his mother, father and older sister arrived and stayed in their small condo. She felt they'd never accepted her; they hadn't attended the wedding. Now, they dominated all her husband's time and although she was trying hard to be understanding, she wanted to be alone with him.

As soon as he died, her pastor and church friends came, bringing food and words of encouragement. She made the necessary arrangements for the funeral. For some reason the funeral home insisted on her paying cash and would not wait for the life insurance to come through with payment. She cleared out their savings account and took care of the expenses.

When they returned from the funeral service, her sister-in-law and mother-in-law packed up all the food friends had brought and took it with them as they left the condo. She didn't know until later that they also took all the cards that friends had left. When a friend said to her, "I hope the $1,000 I put in the card helped with the expenses," she realized that the relatives had kept not only the cards but the cash enclosed also.

She felt hurt, but wanted to give them the benefit of the doubt. So she called the sister-in-law and asked if they picked up the cards. She replied, "Yes" and made no mention of returning them or the money enclosed in some. She just decided to be the bigger person and just ask for a list of the names and addresses so she could send thank you notes.

Hurt and betrayal sliced in on top of her grief—she didn't know what to think. In the weeks to come we worked through the stages of grief: Denial, Anger, Bargaining, Depression/Disorientation, Acceptance. As she went through the necessary adjustments to life alone, she had to release forgiveness again and again.

It wasn't long before her employer began pressuring her to return to work and wanted her to take on a new assignment that would mean more responsibility and longer hours. It seemed that no one was respecting her needs.

Hearing all these things, we had to find out why she was being treated with such insensitivity. We knew that it was important to let the Holy Spirit reveal the roots within her that would account for the betrayal and abandonment. We didn't want to see these patterns repeating in her life.

She was a first-born; her father didn't feel ready for parental responsibilities and quickly disappeared. Her mother was left to make it on her own. Relatives didn't help, and soon her mother found herself a single working mom. Memories of these growing-up years were of always being alone and waiting for her mother to return from work. She became very self-sufficient and performance-oriented. She made good grades and never got into trouble. She worked her way through college and also worked hard at being accepted.

We went through the process of forgiving her father and mother. We dealt with the lies she believed about herself. But then, we asked if she was angry with God for taking her husband. She admitted her life would be a lot happier if her husband had not died. She acknowledged that life and death rested in the hands of God. Then, she said, "Yes, I guess I am. Just as it was with my father, my life would have been a lot happier if he hadn't made the decision to leave before I was born. I guess I'm angry with him too." Now we were getting somewhere. She released forgiveness to God and her father.

Then came the next question, "Are you angry with your husband for dying and abandoning you?" As she cried, "Why did he have to leave me?" the answer gushed forth with her grief. "Yes, I'm angry with him even though it makes no sense." God was cleaning out that deep wound of abandonment so He could heal it once and for all.

We began to see evidence of answered prayers for healing, and I (Shelvy) said to her, "I want you to learn to play and enjoy life. I want you to dream about what you want to do with your life. I give you permission to have a "Pajama Day"—you don't have to get up at any certain time, you don't have to get out of your PJs or get dressed, you don't have do to anything productive, you don't have to answer the phone or door unless you want to, watch a funny movie (laughter is the best medicine) or read a good book. Listen to some good music and just relax."

The next time I saw her, she looked rested and shared with me the new vision she had for her life. A former employee who now worked for a large corporation had contacted her to ask if she was interested in making a job change. As it turned out, she was offered a much better job in a different field that very much interested her and had a more promising future.

She sees God's hand at work in all that is unfolding and is excited about what He has for her. What a blessing to see the changes that poured in once the lies, performance and root of abandonment were removed!

The Story of Three Widows

While I was a widow, I went on a tour of Israel with John and Paula Sandford and a few others. We were at a threshing floor and John read from the book of Ruth, explaining the significance of the harvest as related to that period of time. Someone in our group said to me: "Shelvy, you are a widow like Ruth; stand over on the threshing floor so we can take some pictures to show the size of the threshing floor."

I answered back, "Just make sure there is no Boaz in the picture!"

Later John said to me, "Shelvy, you come and sit with me on the bus; your bitterness is showing." After he lovingly confronted me and prayed for me, he said, "And furthermore, God *does* have a Boaz for you." It was not what I wanted to hear at that time.

In the Old Testament book of Ruth, we find a story of three widows. We have already taken a look at Ruth's story in Chapter One, but let's look again as it portrays different responses to widowhood and the choices faced in those life circumstances:

Naomi was the widow of Elimelech. She and her husband had moved from their homeland, Bethlehem in Judah, because of a famine. Their two sons, Mahlon and Kilion, had traveled with them to the land of Moab where they married Moabite women, Ruth and Orpah. After ten years, all three men had died, leaving all three women widows. Naomi learned that God had come to the aid of His people by providing food in her homeland, and she decided to return home. Her two daughters-in-law loved her and wanted to go with her and help care for her. She told them to stay in their homeland and marry. *"The Lord grant that you will find rest, each in the house of her husband."* (Ruth 1:9)

Orpah kissed her mother-in-law good-by, but Ruth clung to her. Ruth said, *"Entreat me not to leave you or to turn back from following after you; wherever you go I will go, and where you stay I will stay. Your people shall be my people and your God, my God."* (Ruth 1:16)

Two young widows, two choices, two different responses

We never hear of Orpah again and don't know how her life turned out. But as we shared in Chapter One, the story of Ruth is a beautiful love story and a shimmering portrayal of God's betrothal to us. We revisit this story here to highlight the blessing Ruth receives as she chooses to move on in life after loss.

Naomi and Ruth arrive in Bethlehem at the time of the barley harvest. Ruth says to Naomi, *"Please let me go to the field and glean heads of grain after him in whose sight I may find favor."* (Ruth 2:2) She finds herself in the field of Boaz, who was of the clan of Elimelech. Boaz inquires of his foreman, "Whose young woman is this?" The foreman explains who she is, how she had asked permission to glean in the field and had been doing so since morning.

Boaz goes to Ruth and tells her to not go to another field but to stay with his servant girls and his men will not bother her. She bows down and asked "Why have I found such favor in your eyes that you notice me, a foreigner?" Boaz says he's been told about what she's done to help Naomi and how she left her own father and mother and came to live in a land with people she did not know. He blesses her by saying, *"The Lord repay your work, and a full reward be given you by the Lord God of Israel, under whose wings you have come for refuge."* (Ruth 2:12)

At mealtime, Boaz invites her to eat at his table. He is so generous, she has food left over and she takes that home to Naomi. Boaz instructs his men to leave stalks from their bundles of purpose for Ruth to pick up so she won't have to work so hard.

> *It's interesting to note that three times in the book of Ruth, Boaz is with Ruth and he gives to her and never lets her leave empty handed. Love gives! It is said that you can give without loving, but you can't love without giving.*

When Naomi finds out from Ruth what has happened and how she'd been in the field of Boaz, she excitedly tells Ruth, *"This man is a relation of ours, one of our close relatives [a kinsman-redeemer]."* (Ruth 2:20) Ruth continues to glean until the barley and wheat harvests are finished.

In the third chapter, Naomi instructs Ruth, *"Therefore wash yourself and anoint yourself, put on your best garment and go down to the threshing floor; but do not make yourself known to the man until he has finished eating and drinking. Then it shall be, when he lies down, that you shall notice the place where he lies; and you shall go in, uncover his feet, and lie down; and he will tell you what you should do." (Ruth 3:3–4)*

During the night, Boaz is startled to find a woman lying at his feet. *"Who are you?"* he asked. *"I am Ruth, your maidservant,"* she said. *"Take your maidservant under your wing, for you are a close relative." (Ruth 3:9)*

"Blessed are you of the Lord, my daughter!" he replies. *"For you have shown more kindness at the end than at the beginning, in that you did not go after young men, whether poor or rich. And now, my daughter, do not fear. I will do for you all that you request, for all the people of my town know that you are a virtuous woman." (Ruth 3:10–11)*

What an honor that Boaz calls Ruth a virtuous woman, recognizing her noble character. And before she leaves him, He instructs his men, *"Do not let it be known that the woman came to the threshing floor."* (v.14) He's watching out for her reputation. In verse 15 he tells her to bring the shawl she was wearing, and he fills it with barley to take home for her and Naomi.

In chapter four, Boaz redeems the property as kinsman-redeemer and marries Ruth. She gives birth to a son, Obed, who becomes the father of Jesse, the father of David.

For the complete story, read the entire four chapters of the book of Ruth; it's a beautiful story. Who would have ever dreamed that the decision Ruth made as a widow to follow Naomi to a new land would end in such an incredible story of love, loyalty, and lineage!

The Dreaded "C" Word: Cancer

We (Jim and Shelvy) are both dreamers; God speaks to us through dreams. One morning I (Shelvy) woke up with a dream. I wrote it down in my journal and started praying, asking the Lord to tell me what it meant. I didn't tell anyone about the dream. Here is the dream: I went outside to look at the stars at night. As I looked into the sky, I saw a rainbow. I thought, *How can you have a rainbow at night?* I wrote my thoughts concerning the dream: The night speaks of a time of darkness and the rainbow represents the promises of God.

Two days later, I (Jim) woke up with a dream. This is what I told Shelvy: "I dreamed I was looking at the night sky and saw a rainbow. I thought to myself in the dream, *Lord, how can you have a rainbow at night?* To which He moved the rainbow to the side to show me an arc of white sky behind it. I thought, *That is how it would work.*

Now God had our attention and we started to pray! What was God trying to tell us? Were we going to experience a time of darkness and He wanted us to remember His promises?

A long-time friend of Jim's had a dream that Jim was in. In the dream I (Jim) was running down the street and hopped up and sat on top of a red fire hydrant. I then got down and exclaimed, "It will be all right!" and smiled.

I felt this was the third warning that God had given to prepare me. We were both at peace but didn't forget the dreams. We have never had the same dream before. Then I had a regularly scheduled doctor's appointment and told the doctor that I felt something was wrong. The doctor saw that my PSA number had risen a little since the last check-up, and he wanted me to see a Urologist to check everything out. That doctor ordered tests that revealed prostate cancer...the dreaded "C" word that no one wants to hear. But God had prepared us by letting us know there was something ahead where we would need to hold on to His promises. The cancer was caught at a very early stage, thanks to our alert doctor.

While Jim drove us to the hospital every weekday for nine weeks to receive radiation treatments, Shelvy read to him several humorous books. We love to laugh; the Word of God says, *"A merry heart [or laughter] does good, like medicine."* (Proverbs 17:22) Jim had no side effects—not even fatigue. We had many opportunities to minister to patients and their families during our times in the waiting room. Understandably, many were fearful and some were angry. We prayed with a few. Jim made friends with the doctors, nurses and attendants. The last day of his treatments, all of them hugged him. Many said he was the highlight of their day. He would always bring them new jokes. A smile and an encouraging word can go a long way. Always loving with the love of the Lord is irresistible.

Here are some of the promises we prayed and held on to during this time:

- ◆ *"God is faithful, who will not allow you to be tempted beyond what you are able, but … will also make the way of escape, that you may be able to bear it." (1 Corinthians 10:13)*
- ◆ *"I can do all things through Christ who strengthens me." (Philippians 4:13)*
- ◆ *"Be anxious for nothing, but in everything by prayer and supplication, with thanksgiving, let your requests be made known to God and the peace of God, which surpasses all understanding, will guard your hearts and minds through Christ Jesus." (Philippians 4: 6–7)*
- ◆ *"My grace is sufficient for you, for My strength is made perfect in weakness." (2 Corinthians 12:9)*

๛ Prayer

My Lord, I confess I don't understand why some people are healed and others aren't. Forgive me for my anger and all the ways I have blamed You. I choose this day to let God be God and trust in His eternal Love. Only You, Lord know the days ahead and only You can make the decisions concerning life and death. Thank You for Your goodness and mercy toward me. Thank You for Your promise to not put on me more than I can bear. Thank You that Your perfect love cast out all my fear and Your love never fails. In Jesus' name I pray, Amen.

11

From Generation to Generation

Sometimes we see patterns repeating from generation to generation. Scripture shows examples of this.

"...visiting the iniquity of the fathers upon the children to the third and fourth generations." (Deuteronomy 5:9)

Abram and his wife Sarai were about to enter Egypt and he said to her, "Indeed I know that you are a woman of beautiful countenance. Therefore it will happen, when the Egyptians see you, that they will say, 'This is his wife'; and they will kill me, but they will let you live. Please say you are my sister, that it may be well with me for your sake, and that I may live because of you." (Genesis 12:11–13) Because Abram (later changed to Abraham in Gen. 17:5) was *afraid* for *his* life, he asked his wife to lie and say she was his sister.

We see this pattern repeated in the life of their son, Isaac. He had not been born when their incident occurred, but look what happened years later: *And the men of the place asked about his (Isaac's) wife. And he said, "She is my sister," for he was afraid to say, "She is my wife," because he thought, "lest the men of the place kill me for Rebekah, because she is beautiful to behold." (Genesis 26:7)*

Like father, like son. Both let *fear* dictate their actions. Both put their wives in a difficult position. But God is a redeemer and came to the rescue in both cases.

Each family and each nation has its own peculiarities. We receive blessings and we receive curses. Because we deal with people's problems, we have to examine those detrimental traits that are sometimes passed down from generation to generation. For example, we know that statistics reveal that if our parents divorce, that increases the probability that we will also divorce. Just as when we are raised in an alcoholic family, we have a predisposition toward alcoholism as a way of dealing with our pain. Or we marry an alcoholic and we become an enabler. It's interesting to look at some of the nations and observe the various traits for which they are noted. (Our purpose is not to reinforce stereotypes of nationalities, but to point out the relationship between these traits and generational patterns.)

> The drinking and fighting Irish
> The Spanish lover
> The Germans who think they are the superior race
> The Italian with the Madonna complex and a hot temper
> The British who must do things properly

One time Jim and I were traveling and stopped in a British shop. We found a T-shirt that expressed what people believe about our various nationalities. Jim bought it because it was imprinted with the following message:

> "Heaven is where the British are the police,
> The Germans are the mechanics,
> The French are the cooks,
> The Italians are the lovers,
> The Swiss organize everything.
> Hell is where the British are the cooks,
> The Germans are the police,
> The French are the mechanics,
> The Swiss are the lovers,
> and it's all organized by the Italians!"

We still see these influences today. An Italian man told us he grew up knowing his father and uncles all had mistresses. The mistress was put up in an apartment and was treated like a wife; it was usually a long-term relationship. But they would also have girlfriends on the side. The girlfriend would change from time to time, but the man's wife was the mother of his children and honored as such. This information becomes valuable when we are trying to help someone who struggles with infidelity. We don't just look at his behavior but also at "the sins of the fathers."

One of the most outrageous stories we've heard was from a man who had an uncle who lived in the islands. This uncle had fathered several dozen children but had never married. This information came out as we were trying to discover the personal history of this couple. She had one child out of wedlock when she was a teenager. Then her first marriage produced two more children. Meanwhile the husband had fathered several children by different women, out of wedlock. They had a child together and then got married. They had had another child since. They were raising her three children and their own two, plus seeing his other children every other weekend. They had recently given their lives to the Lord and were trying to clean up their "act" and honor God in their marriage. We were trying to help them see how the generations before them had influenced their lives and how the Cross of Jesus Christ could set them free from that influence.

> *We can deceive ourselves by saying we would "never" do the bad things our forefathers did, but Scripture tells us otherwise.*

"[You] say, 'If we had lived in the days of our fathers, we would not have been partakers with them in the blood of the prophets.' Therefore you are witnesses against yourselves that you are sons of those who murdered the prophets. Fill up, then, the measure of your fathers' guilt." (Matthew 23:30–32)

We are all capable of committing every sin possible to man. We lean toward that which is familiar, traditional to our family, our culture and our nationality. To illustrate my point, let me (Shelvy) explain: My mother was an excellent cook. She was noted for her delicious baked hams, so, once I had my own home and wanted to bake a ham, I did all the preparations the way I witnessed my mother doing them. Year after year, I would follow this familiar recipe to get the same delicious results. But one time, I was ready to pour ginger ale over the ham and I stopped to consider, *why ginger ale? Why not some other liquid?* I knew it was to keep the ham moist so it wouldn't dry out, but why ginger ale and not Seven-Up? I grew up seeing my mother do it, so I did the same. I now know it was because of the ginger spice. But my point is that I never questioned it before. There are many things we do because they are familiar or traditional to our family of origin. The way I bake ham is harmless, but many other inherited practices are not.

Generational influences go beyond head knowledge and modeling. We know of a boy and girl who grew up in the same family. Both had been adopted from different birth mothers. After their adoptive parents died, the sister found, among their papers, information concerning their adoptions. She told her brother she wanted to try to find their birth mothers, but he had no interest. He was very bitter against his birth parents and felt that since they had given him away, they obviously wanted nothing to do with him; he wanted to keep it that way. He was a loner, had never married, worked as a bartender and was an unhappy person. Through pursuing the leads, his sister found that his birth mother had been a college student who had become pregnant by a man she met in one of the bars off campus. That man was the bartender!

History Repeating

Let us tell you of a modern day story that has some similarities to King David's.

A woman came for counseling and told us, "I've always tried to be patient and understanding with my husband. He has a very demanding job and travels a lot, even having to be away during holidays. He'll either be home for Christmas Eve or Christmas Day but never both.

"He comes home too tired to do anything with me or our two little girls. I can't even remember the last time we went out on a date. I love him, but sometimes it feels like we aren't connected anymore. Maybe I expect too much; I know his career is important and he does take good care of us. He doesn't want me to work outside the home and I love being available when the girls get home from school. But the truth is,

I'm lonely and I miss the man I married ten years ago. We used to have fun together."

Her background revealed that she was the youngest of three girls. Her mother was a stay-at-home mom and her father worked two jobs. Her father wasn't home much and when he was, he was unavailable emotionally. Her mother told the three girls that he worked very hard and they needed to be quiet when he was home. She said, "You know your father loves you very much."

But *did* she know? We believe a child knows on a heart level that she is loved when she experiences these three things: when the father spends time with her, when the father touches the child with hugs and affection, and when the father talks to the child with words of affirmation and encouragement. We call it the 3Ts: Time, Touch, Talk.

She grew up with little attention or affirmation from the primary man, and then carried that expectation into her marriage. She was pretty content while the girls were home, but when they started school she had too much time on her hands.

We suspected that more was going on than she knew about, or that she was not telling everything. Before praying with her, we asked if she was willing for the Lord to make known to her if there were things "hidden in the darkness." She was willing, because she wanted to fix her marriage.

It wasn't long before she received a call from her husband's corporate office about health insurance. After giving the information requested, the woman on the phone said to her, "Congratulations on the birth of your son!"

This is the story that came out: Her husband had another wife, another family and another home in another state. She was devastated! She wondered, which wife did he marry first? Which one was legal? What other lies had she believed as truth?

As she sobbed the story out to us, she wanted to know what to do. Of course, we could not tell her. We could comfort her, help her sort through her options and assure her that God would be with her each step of the way.

As you can imagine, her husband was relieved that everything was out in the open. It was so stressful living a double life. Now he was left with a big mess to straighten out.

This is his background: His father had come to the United States from another country as a young man in his twenties. He had worked hard to make his way, had married and fathered two children. One of the things his wife admired about him was how he took care of his poor, elderly parents. He sent them money every month and went to visit at least once a year. But years later it was revealed that his father wasn't sending money to his parents but to another wife, another family in another country.

Years later, this son didn't plan on repeating his father's life. "It just happened," he said. "I got involved with a girl through one of my clients and she got pregnant and I felt I had to marry her and take care of her. What else could I do?" he said as he hung his head.

As it turned out, he was legally married to the woman sitting in front of us. And although he went through a marriage ceremony with the other woman, it was not legal.

Both women told him to move out of each living arrangement. Needless to say, both women were hurt; their lives had been turned upside down by a man they thought loved them, only to find out that they had been deceived. Would they ever recover from such betrayal?

He committed to continue financial support for each household. He decided to not see his infant son until he was older and he would completely break with the other woman.

His wife of ten years was a Christian and said she would not file for a divorce right away. She felt their daughters needed regular times with their father and she didn't want to upset them anymore than was necessary. But she didn't honestly know if she could ever trust him again.

She saw Shelvy a few times to work on the healing process, forgiveness, and setting healthy boundaries. She felt that unless he turned his life over to the Lord and became a Christian, the marriage didn't stand much of a chance. Either way, there was a lot of work to do just to have a co-parenting relationship with him. Such was the status of things the last time we saw them.

We don't fully understand all about generational patterns. We know from the scriptures that *the sins of the fathers are visited upon the children* "*to the third and fourth generation,*" *(Exodus 34:7)* but what does that mean? We know it could mean what the fathers model to their children or the children judging and dishonoring their fathers' behavior, but is there more?

Just as we saw history repeating with Abraham and Isaac's treatment of their wives, we also see history repeating with Ishmael being denied the blessing as a firstborn son and the blessing going instead to the second-born, Isaac. Isaac's firstborn was Esau. But Esau did not receive the blessing; his brother Jacob, the second-born son, received the blessing. Different circumstances, but the outcome was the same.

What Is It About 50 Years?

I (Shelvy) have seen a pattern repeating in my family and in the family of my first husband. Let's start with him: He died three months before his fiftieth birthday. He worked in nuclear engineering. His father died before his fiftieth birthday and he was a Naval officer. His father's father died before he turned fifty and he was a maker of violins. As far as we know, none of these men died of some genetic disease passed down through the family.

In my own family, my father died of lung cancer before he turned fifty. He owned a sewing machine business. My father's father worked for the railroad and he was killed in a train accident on his fiftieth birthday.

Who can understand how two people can come together and get married who have the same pattern in their families? Only God knows.

What we usually do is what we saw our parents do. Seldom have we found a person who says, "When I was growing up, I always wanted a marriage just like what my parents had." Usually what we hear is just the opposite. Of course, keep in mind that we are talking to couples whose marriages are in trouble. They are the only ones who come for marriage counseling.

Everyone getting married brings to the altar all their hopes, dreams and expectations. But why doesn't it turn out that way? Have they made inner vows to never have a marriage like that of their parents? Have they decided in their hearts which parent they think was wrong? Did they appoint themselves judge and jury concerning the things that went wrong? Did they violate the first commandment with a promise? ("*Honor your father and mother ...that it may go well with you.*" (*Ephesians 6:1–2*)

Do they need to forgive their parents for the wrong things they modeled about marriage?

> *Even while we don't have the answers to every situation,*
> *we do know that the negative generational patterns can*
> *be broken as we submit to the Lord and live His way.*

❧ Prayer

Father God, Forgive me for every instance in which I have responded in a sinful way when my life has been interrupted. Forgive me for being so quick to blame you. I choose to forgive the generations before me that have influenced my life in a negative way. And I thank you for all the good things that those who have lived before me have brought into my life. In Jesus' name, I pray, Amen.

12

Some Signs That a Marriage May Be in Trouble

No matter how well intended the human efforts, they will fail to produce a healthy marriage. We need the Lord's help and willingness to do marriage His way.

> "A successful marriage is the union between two great forgivers." [1]

The best marriage manual is the Bible. In it we read of those marriage partners who did it right, but also of the many who did it wrong. We can learn from both. Between the two of us we have made a lot of mistakes, but we are happy to say that God is our Redeemer—the God of the second chance!

Below are listed some of the telltale signs that a marriage is in trouble:

- ♦ You begin to focus on the negatives concerning your spouse's behavior while you think less and less about the positive qualities.
- ♦ You are often irritated with your spouse and may speak more harshly or be angrier than is merited.
- ♦ You cease sharing the events of your day with your spouse.
- ♦ You become less interdependent and less corporate with your spouse.

---

[1] (Wall plaque, adapted from a quote by Ruth Bell Graham)

- ◆ You withhold money and become secretive concerning your financial resources.
- ◆ You look for reasons to stay out late, avoiding spending time with your spouse.
- ◆ You are not as sexually active with your spouse as you once were.
- ◆ You begin to spend time with the opposite sex other than your spouse.
- ◆ You no longer pray or worship together.
- ◆ You cease having meals together, going to bed at the same time and/or sleeping together.
- ◆ You no longer go out on dates, weekends away or vacations together.
- ◆ You stop dreaming together.

This is not an exhaustive list and there is no magical number of signs that prove your marriage is in trouble. The truth is, one is too many. A good marriage takes daily work and diligence.

Relationships are difficult at best. But when you add to this the fact you have made a lifetime commitment to one person, have vowed to love him or her in sickness and in health, for richer or for poorer, for better or for worse, you have given that person power in your life (power to lift you up, or to let you down). This commitment is not merely to be made on your wedding day but should be renewed again and again.

We go to school to learn everything from cooking to computers, but nowhere are we taught how to make a marriage work. One time while we were teaching at a marriage retreat, a man came up to us and asked for permission to use the materials we handed out. He was a professor at a prominent university and was planning to offer an elective class on marriage. How delighted we were to be used in a small way to help young people prepare for marriage!

෨ Prayer

Dear God, Forgive me for all the ways I have failed in my marriage. Bring to death in me those wrong concepts of what marriage is all about. I thank You for my spouse. Renew my love and give me Your love to give. Help me understand that it is Your wise plan to have my partner bring out the best in me, but also the worst. You are well acquainted with all my faults and I give You permission this day to make me pleasing in Your sight. Thank You for Your patience to work with me. I recommit myself and my marriage to You. In Jesus' name, Amen.

13

Marriage God's Way

Have you ever turned on to a road and seen a sign printed in bold letters, WRONG WAY? Very quickly, you look for a way to get off that road and on to the right road where you know you will be safe.

When we make a wrong turn, the sooner we acknowledge that, the sooner we will get out of danger and on to the safe road. Sometimes even on the right road, we see a sign, DANGER AHEAD. Then too, it's best to get off that road as soon as possible.

When couples come to us for marriage counseling, sometimes they are headed in the wrong direction. Perhaps they ignored the WRONG WAY sign or even the DANGER AHEAD sign. Like one new couple we saw: On the man's information form, he wrote, "I am currently having an affair; my wife does not know. Please do not tell her."

What is behind these poor decisions? The man we just mentioned was very angry at his wife, and after an hour with her, we understood why.

His affair was a passive aggressive act. Some people get off track when they are looking for greener grass. But when you get up close to that greener grass, you still see the dirt.

Some are looking for a short cut, a more scenic route, or trying to avoid the toll road. The truth is, there are no short cuts or free lunches. For whatever reason we find ourselves on the wrong road or going in the wrong direction, the only way to get home safely is to go back to where we got off the right path.

God is love, and it is love that got us to the altar—the altar for salvation as well as the altar for marriage. Let's return to our first love: Both God and our spouse.

Let's look at some of God's ways for marriage.

1. Commitment

- ◆ Commit your life to live God's way. This enables you to commit to Him and to your spouse.
- ◆ Commit to being purposeful in building a strong marriage, God's way.
- ◆ Commit to spending *time* with your spouse, daily, one on one—being attentive, affectionate and responsive.
- ◆ Commit to a weekly date. Enjoy one another with fun and play and rediscover the wonder of the one you love. Try new things.
- ◆ Commit to a weekend away (without children) every few months.

Commit your way to the Lord, trust also in Him, and He shall bring it to pass. (Psalm 37:5)

I'm afraid the word "commit" doesn't have the same meaning in the 21st Century as it did in years past. One young woman was waiting to walk down the aisle of her wedding with her father when he asked her, "Are you sure you want to do this?" Her reply? "If it doesn't work, we can always get a divorce."

Why is it so hard for some to commit? A man who sat in front of us was one such person. His parents' marriage ended in divorce, as did his own first marriage. Then he had met a woman he loved, and after living together for five years, she said, "Enough is enough! I've been faithful to you, I've made a home for you, I've helped with your children every other weekend and I've helped you get a business started. Now, I want to know where this relationship is going before I invest anymore time into it."

They are newly committed to the Lord go to church every Sunday. They have been living in a way that is acceptable in this time and culture. But what does God say about living together and not being married? Can God really heal the hurts and disappointments of the past?

We say a resounding YES! We'll see where this goes as we teach them of God's forgiveness and His restoration. We are confident that God's love will win them over to do what is pleasing to Him. Only the Spirit can convict of sin.

2. Communication

- Learn to listen with an open mind and an open heart. Keep confidential the secrets of your mate.
- Listen for what your spouse is *not* saying; read body language and tone of voice with compassion, not with eyes and hearts that look for evidence of evil in the other.
- Communicate on a feeling level. Leave little love notes where they'll be found by your mate. Send a text or an email just to say, "I love you and I would marry you all over again."
- Acknowledge your anger with "I" statements. For example: "I feel hurt" instead of, "You hurt my feelings." Or, "I am angry" instead of "You make me so mad." The truth is, no one can make you mad or make you feel a certain way; we choose how we are going to respond to what the other person did. Avoid exploding, or (on the other hand) burying your anger.
- Avoid passive aggressive anger, which could lead to an affair or an affair of the mind (for men, pornography; for women, romance novels and soap operas); these and other activities can be used as ways of getting back at your spouse. When we are angry with our spouse but fail to express it in a healthy way, it will come out sooner or later. If there is no resolution to the behavior of our spouse that has caused us to be angry, anger may come out in passive aggressive behavior. That is not always on a conscience level, but subconsciously we are angry and will do something to get back at the other one. When we do that, we want the other to hurt as much as he has hurt us. It has been our experience, when counseling couples who are involved in affairs, that many are angry with their spouse for various reasons.
- Learn your spouse's "love language." What really makes him or her feel loved? What can you do that will speak to the heart of

your spouse? (Jim knows Shelvy loves to have fresh flowers in the house, so he brings them to her frequently. Shelvy especially appreciates them in the winter when the ground is covered with snow.)

♦ Little gestures can make a big difference. We have a plaque that hangs in our bedroom "Happiness is being married to your best friend."

♦ Verbalize the positive—words of appreciation, affirmation and admiration.

♦ Communicate on a spiritual level. Share what you learn from the Word of God, spiritual dreams, prophetic words and revelations.

♦ Pray together and separately, for each other, for your marriage, for your children, your finances and your needs, and give thanks. Listen for the voice of the Lord together. Worship together.

♦ Communicate sexually that which is mutually satisfying and agreed upon. Learn what pleases your spouse. Make time for this important time of coming together to express your love for one another. Don't let long periods of time lapse without coming together sexually. Don't wait until it's late at night and you are both exhausted. Don't be too busy and too tired. Remember sex was created by God for you to express your love to one another and to become *one*.

Before we were married, during our betrothal period, we would talk for hours and run up huge phone bills. When we were together, it was the same (except without the phone bills!) We wanted to know everything about each other. Then we got married and life happened. We can't remember the last time we talked for hours. We talk, but not for hours.

Now think about being betrothed to the King of Kings. Do we have the same zeal to communicate and spend time with Him? Does He get the first fruits of our day? Do we long for that same intimacy (in-to-me-see)—getting to know Him in greater and greater depths? Do we listen for that quiet, inner voice to hear what He has to say to us? Are we gathering fresh manna each morning so we can feast on His Word? "*Oh, the depth of the riches both of the wisdom and knowledge of God! How unsearchable are His judgments and His ways past finding out!*" (Romans 11: 33)

3. Conflict Resolution

♦ Listen well enough to your partner to be able to feed back what you heard him or her say. Take turns talking and listening.

♦ Brainstorm your options.

♦ Admit when you're wrong and ask for forgiveness.

♦ Take time out when discussion becomes unproductive or too heated. Whoever calls time out needs to take responsibility for resuming the discussion in a timely manner.

♦ Remember, you don't have to be right or have your way all the time. Be willing to give in to your spouse as a sacrificial act of love. (It is unhealthy for one to always do all the giving in.)

♦ Don't part with unresolved differences; (at least set time to discuss and resolve later if you don't have time in the morning). The way a couple separates in the morning will set the tone for the rest of their day.

Never Too Old To Learn

One time Shelvy and I (Jim) were having a discussion. We had a difference of opinion. (We can't even remember what it was about now.) After we had each presented our opinions and view points several times, Shelvy said, "This is unproductive; let's sleep on it and continue talking in the morning. I'm going to bed." I sat there and prayed, "Lord, wasn't I right?"

I heard back, "Yes Jim you were right, but you were wrong." The Lord showed me that while I had all my "ducks in a row" as I laid out the facts, I had not heard Shelvy's heart.

As I asked Shelvy's forgiveness, she said, "It wasn't about who was right; I just wanted you to hear where I was coming from."

I (Shelvy) have no problem following my husband's leadership in a matter, as long as I know he's heard me. I feel it is a wife's responsibility to share her counsel with her husband. If he is wrong, God will intervene, but He cannot bless my disobedience to His Word. I take great comfort in knowing that God is bigger than any mistakes of my husband or mine.

4. Courage

It takes courage to go the distance!

- Encourage one another to come into their full potential, to reach each one's destiny.
- Take time to dream together—no negatives; everything is a possibility. *For with God nothing will be impossible." (Luke 1:37)* God says, "I'm possible!"
- *Wait on the Lord; be of good courage, and He shall strengthen your heart; wait, I say, on the Lord! (Psalm 27:14)*
- When a spouse is discouraged, lift them up with your courage. *"Have I not commanded you? Be strong and of good courage; do not be afraid, nor be dismayed, for the Lord your God is with you wherever you go." (Joshua 1:9)*

5. Corporateness

When a couple marries, they are forming that which never was before. They become a family, just the two of them. They have to leave mother and father to become one flesh. Then the work begins to become corporate: spirit, soul and body. Always be mindful that you have a partner for life. Take him or her into consideration in all your decisions and plans.

Mike Mason, in his book *The Mystery of Marriage*,[1] describes marriage this way:

> *Marriage is like having a huge tree growing in the center of your house. You can't go anywhere without having to take it into consideration, seeing it, going around it, ducking under its branches and sometimes, picking up the mess from the leaves it drops.*

- Share all news with your spouse before sharing it with others.
- Remember two are stronger and more powerful than one.

---

[1] *The Mystery of Marriage*, Mike Mason (copyright 1985, Multnomah Pub., Inc.)

♦ Corporateness is more difficult for men than for women. Women are naturally relational and lean toward dependency. The male is taught to be independent from an early age. When God said, *Leave mother and father, cleave to one another and become one flesh,* that's His formula for oneness. To leave mother and father is not just geographically leaving their house, but it is leaving all dependence on them. The word "cleave" is where we get the word *glue.* Don't let anything pull you two apart!

♦ Be on the alert; Satan's M.O. (*modus operandi*) is always "divide and conquer." And his weapons are "tired" and "busy."

One couple we met with for pre-martial counseling had difficulty deciding if they wanted to have children. One partner had been married before and had children. The other had never been married and definitely wanted the experience of at least one child. We told them this needed to be decided before their commitment of marriage. All they could come to was "maybe" and that meant trouble. After marriage they almost divorced because one definitely wanted a child and one definitely did not. Satan almost won—"divide and conquer."

God's way is oneness: spirit, soul and body! His gifts are grace and mercy.

Just a word about **corporate responsibility:** With all privilege there is responsibility. The blessings that come with marriage also come with responsibility. We must always take the other person into consideration with all our decisions.

Two Biblical examples of corporate responsibility are Daniel and Abigail. Daniel offers us an example of corporate confession and repentance (Daniel 9) *"We have sinned and committed iniquity"* using plural pronouns; we, our and us. Daniel as leader includes himself in corporate confession of sin on behalf of the people.

Abigail says to David, *"On me, my lord, on me let this iniquity be!" "Please forgive the trespass of your maidservant."* (1 Samuel 25) Although it was her husband's decision to treat David and his men so badly, *she* went to David to ask forgiveness.

"For this reason a man shall leave his father and mother and be joined to his wife, and the two shall become one flesh. This is a great mystery, but I

speak concerning Christ and the church. Nevertheless let each one of you in particular so love his own wife as himself, and let the wife see that she respects her husband. (Ephesians 5:31–33)

In Genesis 15–17 God enters into Covenant with Abram. God changes Abram's name: *"No longer shall your name to called Abram, but your name shall be Abraham: for I have made you a father of many nations."* (17:5) In verse 15, God changes Sarai's name to Sarah.

A change of name signifies a change of relationship, as with getting married. We have entered into a covenant. When we become believers in Christ, we are called Christians. In the same manner, when we marry, a woman carries her husband's name and what she does is a reflection on him, good or bad. Her new name tells the world she is in covenant with her husband.

We have found through our years of counseling that if a woman refuses to take her husband's name, there is usually an issue of broken trust in her background. For some reason, she does not want to be corporate or interdependence with the man she is marrying. This is usually accompanied by other decisions of separateness, like keeping their monies and properties separate. Sometimes when a woman is established in a profession and is known as Dr. so & so, she may choose to add her new husband's name with a hyphen onto to her current name.

Only once have we had a situation in which the man took his wife's name when they married. As you might guess, he had big issues with his father and refused to carry his name.

Christ set the example with His bride, the Church. Through Him we have entered into a covenant. It is the same for a man and woman entering into a covenant of marriage.

"Now may the God of peace who brought up our Lord Jesus from the dead, that great Shepherd of the sheep, through the blood of the everlasting <u>covenant</u>, make you complete in every good work to do His will, working in you what is well pleasing in His sight, through Jesus Christ, to whom be glory forever and ever. Amen." (Hebrews 13: 20–21)

❧ Prayer

Lord, I come to you with a broken heart and unfulfilled dreams. My marriage has not turned out the way I thought it would.

Forgive me, Lord, for every way in which I contributed to the dysfunction of my marriage. Forgive me for letting my eyes and my heart stray from the commitment I made before You.

Forgive me for believing the lies that it's better to give up and start over with someone else. Forgive me for the lies I've believed about my spouse and about myself.

Forgive me for blaming You for not fixing my marriage.

I choose this day to be obedient to Your will even before I know what Your will is for my life.

I confess I do not understand about generational patterns. I believe that when Jesus died on the Cross it was for all sin. Break the harmful patterns in my life. In Jesus' name, Amen.

14.

Love Song

There is the King of Kings, Lord of Lords, Holy of Holies and the Song of Songs! The Song of Songs can be read as a song of love from our Beloved to each one of us who love Him. It can also be read as a love letter between a husband and his wife. In it we see history, God's covenant love for His people and also Christ's "bridegroom" love for His Church. Let's look at this love song together. Let's see what the Lord wants to impart to us as we look at the Song of Songs.

*"The Lord your God in your midst, the Mighty One, will save; He will rejoice over you with gladness, He will quiet you with His love, He will rejoice over you with **singing**."* (Zephaniah 3:17)

For many years, it has been my (Shelvy's) practice to read the Bible through in a different translation each year. I had a theology teacher who bought a new Bible each year, to prevent his markings from influencing his interpretations of the Scripture. He shared with the class the prayer he would pray with each new year and each new Bible:

> *"Lord, I release to You all my knowledge, preconceived ideas and beliefs about the scriptures. Enlighten the eyes of my understanding that I may see Your truths fresh and new."*

The best reading plan we have found comes from the book, *Secrets of the Secret Place* by Bob Sorge:[1]

"Divide your daily reading into four sections:

1. Genesis to Malachi (except for Psalms to Song of Solomon): Take that number of pages in your Bible and divide by 365 so that you can read the Old Testament through in one year (3 pages in my Bible).

2. Psalms to Song of Solomon: Count the number of pages in this section and divide by 183 so that you can read it through every six months (1½ pages in my Bible).

3. Matthew through John: Count the number of pages in this section and divide by 183 so that you can read it through every six months (1½ pages in my Bible).

4. Acts to Revelation: Count the number of pages in this section and divide by 183 so that you can read it through every six months. (2 pages in my Bible)."

Studying the Scripture is like looking through a kaleidoscope. Each stone or gem has its individual beauty, its own color. But when you place all the stones together in a kaleidoscope and hold it up to the light, you see a design of breathtaking beauty and with each turn, another design more beautiful than the last. That's the way reading the Bible is, and especially as I have read the Song of Songs through the years. As I change and mature, I see something different each time in those sacred verses of Scripture.

I want to glean new thoughts, new revelations and never have a mindset that I know what a particular verse means. I want the Lord to take me deeper and deeper into His truths. I have this verse from Isaiah 50:4–5 written in the back flyleaf of my Bible: *The Lord God has given me the tongue of the learned, that I should know how to speak a word in season to Him who is weary. He awakens me morning by morning. He awakens*

---

[1] Oasis House, P.O. Box 522, Grandview, MO 64030-0522, Missouri, copyright 2001, page 77.

my ear to hear as the learned. The Lord God has opened my ear; and I was not rebellious, nor did I turn away." This verse is my prayer.

I have been a child, a teenager, a young woman, a married woman, a mother, a widow, and now, a more mature wife and servant of the Lord. I approach the Song of Songs from the perspective of being betrothed to the King. It is more endearing to me as I read it first of all as God's love letter to me. It is the cry of my heart—as was the Shulamite maiden's in Chapter One—for His kiss of intimacy, for the intoxication of His love that is better than wine, and for an experience of the fullness of His name. Her prayer is, *"Draw me away!"* She says, *"The king has brought me into his chambers."* (*Song of Songs 1:4*) "His chambers" is a place of intimacy—the secret place of the Most High.

"One thing I have desired of the Lord, that will I seek: that I may dwell in the house of the Lord all the days of my life, to behold the beauty of the Lord, and to inquire in His temple. For in the time of trouble He shall hide me in His pavilion; in the secret place of His tabernacle He shall hide me; He shall set me high upon a rock." (*Psalm 27:4–5*)

I want to be found trustworthy with whom the Lord can share His secrets.

Just as the Shulamite maiden wanted His name, she wanted all that it represented, the power and authority, the security and privilege. But with that name goes the responsibility as well. How many times have we heard the venomous words, "You call yourself a Christian?"

The first time I married, as a young woman I can recall having to change a few records to carry my new name, but then what a difference the second time! It was 30 years later and much had been established. I began with changing my personal identification in my wallet. Then I set out to have the following changed: Social Security, all properties (titles, deeds, car registrations), tax returns, credit cards, bank accounts, library card, life insurance polices, passport, auto club, warehouse clubs, super market cards, business card, check cashing card, church roll, telephone directory, business and club memberships, magazine and book subscriptions, luggage name tags, postal service, personal and business stationery—and so much more that I lost count.

There may have been others, but those were enough to make any woman think twice about giving up her name. I can remember feeling overwhelmed and with each change, thinking, "I'm in too deep now to turn around and go back. This better be God or I'm done for!"

I want to carry the name of Christ in an honorable way. I am thankful for the privilege to use that name to call upon the Lord and I take very seriously the responsibility of the power and authority that goes with His name. Just as everything I do and say is a reflection on my husband (because I carry his name), so it is with being called a Christian. I don't ever want to bring shame on His name.

In the first chapter, ninth verse of the Song of Songs, the Beloved calls her, *fairest among women, my love.* He compares her to His *filly among Pharaoh's chariots.* Before you women take offence at being compared to a horse, let me remind you that today that would be like your husband comparing you to his beloved pickup truck, or to his new sport or luxury car. Does that make you feel better? You know how he loves his "wheels."

In all fairness, the Beloved goes on to say to her, *"Behold, you are fair, my love, you are fair. You have dove's eyes." (Song of Songs 1:15)* He has won her heart, because her response is, *"You are handsome, my beloved." (v.16)* But she continues, since she is thinking corporately: **Our** *bed... our houses... and* **our** *rafters. (v.17)* She wants to be **one** with her beloved.

In Chapter Two of Song, she proclaims, *"His banner over me is love." (v.4)* The Beloved has brought her into His banqueting house, and there for all to see is the flag He has raised to honor the one He loves. He has conquered her heart. It cost Jesus dearly to raise His banner of love over us. *Now Pilate wrote a title and put it on the cross. The title read, JESUS OF NAZARETH, KING OF THE JEWS. Then many of the Jews read this title, for the place where Jesus was crucified was near the city, and it was written in Hebrew, Greek, and Latin. (John 19:19–20)*

The Beloved invites her, *"Rise up, my love, my fair one and come away, for lo, the winter is past, the rain is over and gone. The flowers appear on the earth; the time of singing has come, and the voice of the turtledove is heard in our land. The fig tree puts forth her green figs, and the vines with the tender grapes give a good smell. Rise up, my love, my fair one, and come away!" (Song of Songs 2:10–13)* What a picture of springtime. A time of resurrection for all that has been dormant through the cold, harsh winters of our lives.

As we pen this chapter, we are visiting our friends' waterside cottage on Prince Edward Island. It is early June; the snow and ice of winter have melted and the boarded-up windows are being uncovered. Life is stirring and birds are singing. Boats are emerging from under heavy tarpaulins from winter storage. The purple and pink lupines are resurrected from what was frozen earth, now thawed by the sun. Signs of new life are everywhere. May we all experience resurrection renewal!

May the warmth of the Son, bringing God's Presence, thaw the cold hardness of our hearts with the reality of His love. May we bloom right where we are planted and come forth bearing much fruit in our lives. May we give off a sweet fragrance of His resurrected life from within our transformed hearts.

In Chapter Two of Song of Songs, His invitation continues, "O my *dove, in the clefts of the rock, in the secret places of the cliff, let me see your face, let me hear your voice; for your voice is sweet, and your face is lovely."* (v. 14) She responds, *"My beloved is mine, and I am his."* (v. 16)

Jesus is our Rock and the cleft in the rock is His pierced side, out of which flowed blood and water. He was giving birth to the Church. He invites us to come to that secret place of His wounded side. He wants to see *our* face that He calls lovely and hear *our* voice that He says is sweet! True prayer is a dialogue between two who love each other. Our love matters to the Lord! Just as we love to hear His words of love to us, He wants to hear those words of love and admiration back to Him.

I have encouraged every person I have mentored through the years to keep a journal. It is important to nail down those special thoughts from the Lord. And how it builds our faith as God speaks through dreams and prophetic words to us. Recently, after a glorious time with the Lord and in the Word, I felt Him say, "Go lie down and go to sleep, I want to speak to you." I lay down at 8:35 am and woke up at 9:09 am with a very meaningful dream. In fact, the dream revealed the answer to something I had been asking Him about for some time.

I cherish those quiet times in the secret place of His Spirit, where He speaks those words of love to my inner man. When the words are a lot smarter than I am, I know they come from the Lord. Like the times

I hear unfamiliar words, which I can't spell or define; I go in search for the dictionary. What a joy to be as Mary of Bethany and sit at His feet and learn of Him!

As I read Chapter Three of Song of Songs, I can identify with her troubled night. I think of the book *Dark Night of the Soul*[2] in which Saint John of the Cross wrote of his experience. These writings helped me understand what I had been going through so many years earlier, in that period of testing in my life. It was a time when I couldn't sense God's presence. I felt my prayers were going no higher than the ceiling. I questioned my salvation. I questioned the Bible. I questioned the very existence of God Himself. None of it seemed real to me. I thought, *Maybe it's all just my imagination and none of this "faith business" is real.* Like the Shulamite maiden, *I sought Him but I did not find Him. (v. 1)* What I finally came to was this: "Lord, if You are not real and this is all some figment of my imagination and I'm actually losing my mind, I choose to hold on to belief in You anyway. Even if they eventually haul me off to the insane asylum, I choose to believe that You will never leave me nor forsake me." I have experienced the Dark Night of the Soul and He is faithful and never puts on us more than we can bear. Then my soul was at peace. That time of testing was over.

In the book *More Than Words*, Keith Miller describes this season of our life:

"God follows a pattern of revealing Himself and then silence. He has not "gone" as many seem to think, but rather is giving us the chance to act in faith; the freedom to follow with fidelity what we have been given, or to turn and run as prodigals, or to return and surrender to a new phase of the growth of the person."[3]

When I was a little girl, there was a song we used to sing in church:

"I have decided to follow Jesus,
No turning back, no turning back.

---

[2] St. John of the Cross (1542-1591) - *Dark Night of the Soul* (orig. copyright 1953 Newman Press; Dover Pub. 2003)
[3] *More Than Words* J. Keith Miller (copyright 2002 Baker Books)

The world behind me, the cross before me
No turning back, no turning back.
Though none go with me,
Still I will follow." [4]

("No turning back"—that was the resolve I came to.)

Every relationship – friendships and especially every marriage relationship – goes through times of testing. I remember, in the early months of marriage to Jim, thinking, "This is the biggest mistake of my life!" I had to give up too much—home, family, friends, church, my beloved bookstore and a lifelong pension that gave me financial security. I've heard it said that we should not dwell on the cost of obedience but rather on the high cost of disobedience! A friend of ours used to say, "I didn't sign on for this!"

But testing is not always a bad thing. When I drive an automobile, I want to know it's been tested. I want any medication I take to be well scrutinized, too. Randy Alcorn in his novel *Safely Home* tells of the persecuted church in China and makes this statement through the sage in the story: "Real gold fears no fire."[5] May we be "real gold," trusting Him in the times of testing, when things in our lives are heating up and trouble is brewing.

In Song of Songs Chapter Four, the Beloved is quite the man with words. No less than five times he calls her, *My spouse.* All the while praising her: *"You are fair, my love!"* (v. 1) He waxes poetic about her eyes, hair, teeth, lips, mouth, temples, neck and breasts. Solomon writes in Proverbs 5:19, *As a loving deer and a graceful doe, let her breasts satisfy you at all times; and always be enraptured with her love.* In Song of Songs 4:9 He proclaims twice: *"You have ravished my heart."* Then he speaks of her fragrance. This reminds me of 2 Corinthians 2:14–15: *Now thanks be to God who always leads us in triumph in Christ, and through us manifests the fragrance of His knowledge in every place, for we are to God the fragrance of Christ.* In other words, we come away bearing the fragrance of whomever we have recently embraced.

---

[4] Lyrics attr. to S. Sundar Singh (public domain)
[5] *Safely Home*, Randy Alcorn (copyright 2001 Tyndale House)

The Shulamite's Beloved continues to pour out his heart of love for her as he describes her as a garden, a spring, a fountain, as plants, fruits, spices, a fountain of gardens, a well of living waters, and streams from Lebanon. What a picture of LIFE! Her response is to cry out to the winds of the Spirit to blow upon her garden, that its spices may flow out. *"Let my beloved come to his garden."* (Song of Songs 4:16). Note that she no longer calls it **her** garden but **his** garden.

He who believes in Me, as the scripture has said, out of his heart will flow rivers of living water. (John 7:38)

Oneness is pictured in Chapter 5 as the Beloved responds; *"I have come to my garden, my sister, my spouse."* (v. 1)

The "lovesick" maiden describes her Beloved as *Chief among ten-thousand.* (v. 10) She brings out her poetic side as she exalts his head, locks, eyes, cheeks, lips, hands, body, legs, countenance, mouth: *"...he is altogether lovely. This is my beloved. And this is my friend."* (v. 16) It is a wonderful thing to be able to call your spouse your friend! One of my cherished gifts from Jim is a small plaque that hangs in our bedroom, "Happiness is being married to your best friend."

In Chapter 6 of Song, the Shulamite maiden sounds like a woman who knows she is loved. *I am my beloved's and my beloved is mine.* That statement has a ring of security in it. She has found her identification in the one who loves her, our great "I AM!"

Dear one, do you know that you are loved? Jesus loved you so much He stretched out His arms to demonstrate how much when He was nailed to the Cross.

In verse 4, the Beloved praises the Shulamite's beauty: *"O my love, you are beautiful ... lovely...awesome as an army with banners!"* He says this phrase twice in this chapter.

This reminds me of a dream I had some years ago: a bride dressed in a beautiful white wedding gown lifted up her dress so she could walk. When she did that, it revealed that she was wearing combat boots! The dream reminded me that while we are the Bride of Christ and we are clothed in His righteousness, we also are in a battle; our warfare is with the enemy of our souls.

An interesting thing happens in Chapter Seven, where we read of the Beloved again praising her beauty. He begins with her feet, then thighs, navel, waist, breasts, neck, eyes, nose, head and hair. Why would he start with her feet? Earlier in their relationship, he always began at the top with her head.

> *I believe that as we mature, we are more attracted to the* **character** *of a person; their* **daily walk** *is more important than how their face looks. Outer beauty can fade, but inner beauty is enduring.*

Do not let your adornment be merely outward, arranging the hair, wearing gold, or putting on fine apparel, rather let it be the **hidden person of the heart,** *with the incorruptible beauty of a gentle and quiet spirit, which is very precious in the sight of God. (1 Peter 3:3–4)*

Let's pray with the apostle Paul in Colossians 1:9–10, *that you may be filled with the knowledge of His will in all wisdom and spiritual understanding; that you may* **walk** *worthy of the Lord, fully pleasing Him, being fruitful in every good work and increasing in the knowledge of God.*

And also as in Ephesians 5:1–2, *Therefore be imitators of God as dear children. And* **walk** *in love, as Christ also has loved us and given Himself for us, an offering and a sacrifice to God for a sweet-smelling aroma.*

God does all things with meaning and purpose, and most of the time we don't know the half of it when it is happening. I look back at that memorable time before we were married, when the Lord told Jim to wash my feet. He thought he was being obedient to the Lord's instruction because I was one who ministered to others and he was honoring me as one whose feet got "dirty" in service for the Lord. I thought the reason Jim was washing my feet was to confirm the Ephesians 5 passage the Lord had given to me, *that the husband was to wash the wife with the water of the Word.* There was more to it than either of us knew. He later told me that he was first attracted to me because of my **walk** with the Lord. He saw me as a woman of substance.

The Lord set our wedding day as the Thursday before Easter. It was on Thursday before the crucifixion and resurrection that Jesus washed the feet of His disciples. The Apostle John recorded the scene in Chapter 13 of the gospel that bears his name. What a picture of humility: the work of a lowly servant (most likely a slave) doing the dirty job. Jesus didn't think it was beneath His dignity. He was always the Teacher by His actions and by His words. He had no concerns about marring His reputation. He knew Who He was and Whose He was. He also knew His time had come. He Who created time…was running out of time! The Cross awaited Him. He washed His disciples' feet because He loved them, and loved them through to the end. He washed the feet of every one of them, even Judas.

> *What love was it that enabled Him to bow before the one who already had it in his heart to betray Him! Only the love of God in our hearts can enable us to humble ourselves with the attitude of a foot-washer even to those who would betray us.*

> *In washing the feet of the disciples, Jesus was saying, "Watch your **walk**. How's your **character**? How are your attitudes toward one another?"*

An artist and creative director for a New York advertising firm, Ian Shields was a good friend of Jim's for several years. It was during this time that he was in an auto accident and received a severe injury to his arm. While in rehabilitation, he began woodcarving to exercise his arm. Not only did he discover a piece of art inside each piece of wood just waiting to be released, he also found that there was a sculptor inside of him being set free to create beautiful works of art. We are privileged to own some of those works of art. Among our treasures is a rubbing of Ian's woodcarving entitled, "Jesus Washes the Feet of the Disciples." We have this beautifully framed piece hanging in a place of honor in our home. It reminds us of that precious prophetic act when the Lord had Jim wash my feet, and also a reminder that we are to maintain an attitude of being one who washes the feet of others.

Another interesting thing occurs in this seventh chapter of Song of Songs – He sees the whole person and refers to her *stature*. He loves all of her, everything about her. That reminds us of the scripture that admonishes us to mature to the full stature that is found in Christ. Now the Beloved is even more intimate in his verbal lovemaking: "*Let now your breasts be like clusters of the vine, the fragrance of your breath like apples, and the roof of your mouth like the best wine.* She matches his words of love with, *I am my Beloved's and his desire is toward me. Come, my beloved, let us go … let us lodge … let us get up early … let us see …There I will give you my love.*" Observe the plural pronoun "us," signifying mutuality in love.

In Chapter Eight, the Shulamite maiden is seen by others as she leans on her Beloved. Are we willing to be that dependent on our Beloved, to let Him be our heavenly crutch? It reminds me of another who was not ashamed to lean on Jesus. *Now there was leaning on Jesus' bosom one of His disciples, whom Jesus loved. (John13:23)* We know that John was referring to himself as the one that Jesus loved.

In verse 6, she says to her Beloved, "*Set me as a seal upon your heart, as a seal upon your arm; for love is as strong as death.*" And in verse 7: "*Many waters cannot quench love, nor can the floods drown it. If a man would give for love all the wealth of his house, it would be utterly despised.*" A seal of approval, a seal of ownership, a seal of authority and a seal of authenticity set on the inner man of his heart and the outer man of his arm, his strength. The strength of death is that it is inevitable, unstoppable. It is appointed unto every man once to die. God is love and His love can't be quenched, it can't be drowned. *For our God is a consuming fire. (Hebrews 12:29)*

The Shulamite maiden said, *I became in His eyes as one who found peace (v,10)* She found peace in this relationship with her Beloved. She has gone through testing and has counted the cost. She is at peace!

He Himself is our peace. (Ephesians 2:14)

One of the names for Jesus, mentioned in Isaiah 9:6, is *Prince of Peace.* We can't make ourselves be at peace. We can't work it up, or create that place of peace. It is in opening our hearts for the Prince of Peace to come in and take up residence that we are at peace.

Peace I leave with you. My peace I give to you; not as the world gives do I give to you. Let not your heart be troubled, neither let it be afraid. (John 14:27)

These things I have spoken to you, that in Me you may have peace. In the world you will have tribulation; but be of good cheer, I have overcome the world. (John 16:33)

The last recorded words of the Beloved to the one He loves are, "Let Me hear your voice." (Song of Songs

*8:13) He wants to talk with her, to hear her voice. This
is a call to prayer! Our Lord wants to hear from us!*

May His heavenly computer screen always say, "You got mail!" Do
you remember when you first fell in love and you could talk for hours
with your beloved? Then you got married and somewhere along the way
you just stopped talking as much. What happened? Is the Lord calling
you to return to your first love?

Nevertheless I have this against you, that your have left your first love.
(Revelation 2:4) He's waiting and wants to hear your voice. The last
thing she says to her Beloved is, *"Make haste, My Beloved!" (v. 14)* I am
reminded of Abigail when David sent for her to become his wife, *"She
made haste! (1 Samuel 25:42)*

Our desire is to be reunited with the one we love! *"And the Spirit and
the bride say, 'Come!' and let him who hears say, 'Come!'" (Revelation 22:17)*

Love has won the heart of the Shulamite maiden. **Love** has brought
her through a season of testing. **Love** is stronger than death. **Love** melts
the hardest of hearts. The **love** of *our* God never fails!

Richard Wurmbrand writes on his concluding page in his book, *The
Sweetest Song*, "I could not make words convey what happens between
the Bridegroom and the bride, for the same reason that you cannot
weigh granite columns in pharmaceutical scales. Solomon could not do
it, so I most certainly cannot." [6]

Some things just have to be experienced. The Song of Songs is a good
start but there is so much more. Each of us has to enter individually into
that intimate love relationship with the Bridegroom to know personally
the fullness of His love.

We are reminded of an excellent teacher on the Song of Solomon,
Dr. Donald Pickerell, professor LIFE Bible College, San Dimas, CA. He
is the brother of Judy French. Dick and Judy French are international
ministers in the Body of Christ and have been good friends of ours for
many years. Dr. Pickerell says, "The Song itself is like its favorite fruit,
pomegranates, alive with color and full of seeds." [7] Our prayer is that

[6] *The Sweetest Song*, Richard Wurmbrand (copyright 1993 Living Sacrifice Book Co.)
[7] Teaching by Donald Pickerell, Professor, LIFE Bible College, San Dimas, CA

you have come away from this brief look at the Song of Songs with many seeds for thought. May they all bear much fruit!

❧ Prayer

King of Kings, Lord of Lords, Lover of my soul,
    Thank You for Your love letters to me.
    Thank You for parting the veil a little that I might see You in greater clarity. You have created in me a hunger to know you more.
    Thank You for the continual feast as I sit at Your table to partake of the manna You so generously give.
    I love you, my Lord and desire to love you more. In Jesus' name I pray, Amen.

    P.S.

We would like to add a postscript: At the beginning of 2013, the Lord imparted an idea we never thought before, never read about, never heard in a teaching or sermon. He said, "I want you to give Me a tithe of your time. Every day I want you to spend 10% of your day with Me. So we figured it up: 24 hours in a day, 60 minutes in each hour, equals 1,440 minutes in a day. We felt the Lord was saying to give Him 2 hours and 24 minutes every day in His Holy Presence, in the Word and in prayer, listening as well as making requests.

We honestly thought, *How can we do it?* We counsel 40 hours a week, go to the Fitness Center 5 days week for one hour, do the chores that need to be done to keep a house and ministry running in a responsible manner. So our prayer was, "Lord, if you will make the time, wake us up and show us how to make it happen, we are willing." He is faithful! This has been the richest time of our lives. At the end of the first year, four journals were filled with incredible revelations, dream and visions, exchanges of love and so much more than we could have possibly asked for.

    Listen!
    Our Lord is saying, "Come, My Beloved, My Betrothed one. I'm waiting for you in our Secret Place."

Bibliography

Chapter One

(1) New Spirit-Filled Life Bible, p. 1114 (2024 Thomas Nelson)
(2) *Secrets of The Secret Place,* Bob Sorge, 2001 Oasis House, p 185
(3) *Counterfeit Gods,* Timothy Keller Riverhead Books, Penguin Group Introduction pp XXVI

Chapter Three

(1) More Than Words, J. Keith Miller (2002 Baker Books)

Chapter Six

(1) "Serenity" Prayer, Reinhold Niebuhr (circa 1933)

Chapter Twelve

(1) The Mystery of Marriage, Mike Mason, 1985 Multnomah Pub. Inc.

Chapter Thirteen

(1) Secrets of The Secret Place, Bob Sorge, Ibid. pp 170-171
(2) *Dark Night of the Soul,* Saint John of The Cross (1542-1591) (Orig. 1953 New Man Press; 2003 Dover pub.)
(3) *More Than Words,* J. Keith Miller, Ibid.
(4) "I Have Decided To Follow Jesus," song by S. Sundar Sing

(5) *Safely Home*, Randy Alcorn (2001 Tyndale House)

(6) *The Sweetest Song*, Richard Wurmbrand

(7) Song of Solomon, Dr. Donald Pickerell, Professor: LIFE Bible College, San Dimas, Ca.

Watch for future books to be released
in *The Courtship of God* series:

In the third book in this series, you will find how God gives a vision and then gives the provision for fulfilling it. We will be sharing about how we have lived by faith for almost three decades. We have never charged a set fee for our counseling sessions or for teaching and speaking engagements. The Lord showed us early on that we were to allow people to give what they believed they could afford. We have discovered that God is the first Giver. God is love and love always gives. We are called to tap into his unlimited resources so that we too can become givers with His heart and His vision. Provision is not just about money or miraculous abundance, but about knowing that God is *for* us and learning His principles regarding giving and receiving. It is also about aligning with those principles, entering into right relationship from which we can express His love to others with what we've received.

The fourth book will be about the mysteries of God and how they are recognized today. We reveal some of the ways God's heavenly kingdom has wonderful treasures for us to explore while here on earth. See how the Lord also uses many other love languages to reach us: dreams, visions, prophecy, words of knowledge, signs, parables, puzzles, mysteries of all kinds. He writes on the circumstances of our lives with His unique handwriting. Because of His love, He is not silent but speaks in a myriad of ways. Wisdom comes as we learn how to discern and handle this information in a responsible manner.

Our prayer is that through each book, you the reader will be drawn into God's great heart of love. You will enter into a greater depth in your love relationship with Him. As you discover how much He loves you and opens your eyes to see how He is courting you. This is all about the Courtship of God.

You are Betrothed To The King!

Printed in the United States
By Bookmasters